Ford PICKUP TRUCKS 1948-56

Development history and restoration guide

Paul G. McLaughlin

Motorbooks International
Publishers & Wholesalers Inc
Osceola, Wisconsin 54020, USA ®

MW00844519

First published in 1986 by Motorbooks International Publishers & Wholesalers Inc, PO Box 2, 729 Prospect Avenue, Osceola, WI 54020 USA

© Paul G. McLaughlin, 1986

All rights reserved. With the exception of quoting brief passages for the purposes of review no part of this publication may be reproduced without prior written permission from the publisher

Motorbooks International is a certified trademark registered with the United States Patent Office

Printed and bound in the United States of America

The information in this book is true and complete to the best of our knowledge. All recommendations are made without any guarantee on the part of the author or publisher, who also disclaim any liability incurred in connection with the use of this data or specific details

Library of Congress Cataloging-in-Publication Data

McLaughlin, Paul G.
Ford pickup trucks, 1948-56.

1. Ford trucks—History. 2. Trucks—Conservation and restoration. I. Title.
TL230.5.F57M38 1986 629.2'23 86-7039
ISBN 0-87938-213-9 (pbk.)

Cover photograph: 1956 Ford F-100, owned by Jim Petersen

Motorbooks International books are also available at discounts in bulk quantity for industrial or sales-promotional use. For details write to Special Sales Manager at the Publisher's address

Dedication

To my dad, Paul McLaughlin, and the late Dan Mahoney, two Ford truck salesmen who started my affection for Ford trucks with a ride back in 1955 in a new F-100 pickup.

Contents

Acknowledgments

One can't put together a book like this without the help of others. I would like to take this opportunity to thank the following people: Applegate & Applegate Photographs; Jim and Joyce Clements; Dave Crippen, The Ford Archives; Ford Motor Company; Ford Photographic Services, Ford Motor Company; Gene Makrancy, The Ranchero Club; Bernice McLaughlin; Frances I. McLaughlin; Paul G. McLaughlin, Elbery Motor Company, Inc.; Howard Montgomery, The Ford Federation; Irvin Neubert, Light Commercial Vehicle Association; Cynthia Read-Miller, The Ford Archives; Herman Smith, Historical Consultant, Ford Motor Company of Canada; Archie Stutt; Larry Weis, Truck Division, Ford Public Relations.

Introduction

The future looks very bright for growing interest in Ford commercial vehicles of this era. Every day it seems that more trucking enthusiasts are falling under the spell and charms of these trucks. Many feel that they are at, or near, the top of any list that ranks Ford trucks, and some even think they may be the best Ford trucks ever made. There is no denying that these trucks are the most popular ever made by Ford, judging by the number of enthusiasts that stand behind them.

For years, the primary interest in this hobby segment has been generated by and for the "classic" 1953-56 F-100 series. But changes are coming. Interest is starting to grow for the earlier, 1948-52, series. Also, enthusiasts are not only interested in half-ton-model pickups; we are starting to see more panel vans, three-quarter-ton trucks and other nonpickup vehicles being shown at truck shows. And the number of restored vehicles being shown is increasing. Although the legion of modified vehicles and fans remains strong, it's refreshing to see stock trucks being displayed. This is a trend I hope to see continue.

Chapter 1

Looking back: the early years, 1948-52

World War II had just ended in 1945, and the American automobile assembly lines were being cranked up to resume civilian production. Americans had not been allowed to buy new cars for the war's duration, and after four long, carless years, they were standing in line with cash in hand.

What went for cars also could be said for trucks—especially trucks that fell in the light-duty category (pickup trucks and related vehicles). Buyers needed these vehicles just as much as they needed new cars, so the manufacturers easily sold every one they built. However, the manufacturers knew these happy days wouldn't last forever. If dealers wanted to keep their customers they'd better have something new available when demand for those prewar designs diminished.

Ford Motor Company, the nation's number-three car maker at that time, was nearly on the rocks when the war came to a close. When Henry Ford II took over in 1945 he decided to revamp the whole company and all its products. He felt the only thing that could revitalize the ailing company was to offer the public a new, dramatically styled vehicle that would place Ford in the role of leadership and prove that its product wasn't behind the times. The word went out to Styling and Engineering to come up with something that would take Ford out of the thirties and propel it into the fifties and beyond.

Henry Ford had steadfastly refused to make changes for change's sake while other manufacturers had continually changed their vehicles, at least on the surface, so people perceived them as something new, when they were really only in a different wrapper. It worked for the other companies and Henry Ford II felt it would work for Ford too, so he decided to break out of his grandfather's mold. Following his directives, late in 1945 new sketches were shown and approved, and the die was cast for the new Lincoln, Mercury, Ford and 1948 Ford truck line.

1948

The newly designed Ford trucks beat the Ford cars to market by a full five months, arriving on January 16, 1948. The cars were called 1949 models but the trucks were designated as 1948 models. (Ford wasn't the only company with newly designed trucks in 1948; Chevrolet, GM and Dodge also released new designs.)

This complete redesign was the first revamping in a decade, and was quite well

"Bonus Built" was a popular advertising slogan that Ford copywriters used throughout the 1948-52 period.

received as Ford's first postwar effort. To tie the whole line together as one package, for the first time, a common cab was used throughout—from the lightest model to the heaviest. Ford had some financial woes at the time and sharing components meant a per-unit savings that netted a better dollar return.

The redesign cost Ford lots of money and it was a daring move to make. If Ford had decided to play it safe and stay with the same designs we might not have these vehicles with us today. Though the cars and trucks proved to be successful, Ford was locked into the designs for a few years to recover its expenses.

Ford offered three new Bonus Built pickup versions in 1948 (Bonus Built was a marketing term coined by Ford's copywriters to indicate to the customer that Ford added something extra to the trucks). In the half-ton range, Ford offered a new series called the F-1, which was available with a 6½ foot bed, a platform body, a stake body, a cab-and-chassis version, a panel van, a chassis-and-cowl version (to which the customer could add his or her own body) or a chassis-cowl-windshield version (also for a customer-supplied body). Chassis-and-cowl versions were quite popular as door-to-door delivery vehicles. In my neighborhood, the milkman had one, and the Hostess Bakery man had one that we would follow practically every morning. The ice cream man who came around at night had one too, with a special icebox body built on the back.

Moving up the scale brings us to the next designation, the F-2, which was nominally rated as a three-quarter-ton (nominally rated means that these trucks were built stronger than their three-quarter-ton rating, in order to give their owners many years of dependable

Though not as popular as their Ford or Chevrolet counterparts, the Studebakers of the 1949-56 period were nice-looking pickup trucks, as evidenced by this factory promotional photograph. Changes were so minimal that it's difficult to date this photo. Applegate & Applegate

Chevrolet produced some handsome trucks during the 1948-55 period that provided worthy competition to their Ford counterparts. (This is probably a 1952 or 1953 model.) Applegate & Applegate

Pre-1948 pickups are easily distinguished from the later ones by noting changes in the cab, hood, fenders and grille. Applegate & Applegate

service). In this series, the base model was offered with an eight-foot express body, which gave its owner a little more carrying capacity. Almost all the offerings in the F-1 series were also available in the F-2 series except for the panel van. The F-1 was placed on a 114 inch wheelbase; the F-2's wheelbase was stretched eight inches, to 122. Other differences found between the two series were in wheel sizes, springs, tires, clutches and rear axles—all were stronger than in their lighter-rated brothers. If the F-2 wasn't heavy-duty enough for you, Ford offered a three-quarter-ton heavy-duty model called the F-3. These trucks were built with stronger parts and equipment than the F-2s.

Prior to 1948, if you wanted to buy a Ford light commercial vehicle, you had two choices: You could pick a half-ton-rated model or you could choose a larger, one-ton-rated vehicle, appropriately called a Tonner. When the new Ford trucks were introduced into the 1948 market, buyers had more models and ratings to choose from. The half-ton models returned under the F-1 designation, while two new three-quarter-ton models were introduced under the F-2 and F-3 designations. The F-2 was a light-duty three-quarter-ton,

The 1948 pickups look taller, wider and a bit longer than their predecessors, as this 1948 F-1 half-ton shows. Ford Motor Company

while the F-3 was a heavy-duty three-quarter-ton with a gross vehicle rating higher than the earlier one-ton series. Ford still offered a Tonner under the F-4 designation; though Ford still listed it as a light-duty model, it was promoted as a medium-duty model. The F-4 Tonner stayed in the Ford truck lineup through 1952, when Ford dropped the designation and the Tonner title.

Ford offered a total of thirty-eight models in the three light-duty series, virtually something for everyone.

In the power department two engines were offered. One was a six-cylinder called the Cost Clipper (to denote how economical it was to operate) that carried an advertised rating of ninety-five horsepower. It was of an L-head design, displacing 226 cubic inches, and offered plenty of torque for load carrying, as well as the potential for fuel savings. On the other side of the coin, Ford offered its 239 cubic inch V-8, the famous flathead engine that offered a full 100 horses for extra pulling power.

Both engines were known to give many years of dependable service. The sixes carried an 8H designation while the V-8s carried an 8R code and another code designating

LOOKING

FOR A GOOD USED TRUCK?

Your best used truck *value* is an A-1 Used Truck from your Ford Dealer. He has a *big selection* of used trucks . . . with plenty of unused miles in them!

See your reliable FORD Dealer . . . He's the only one who has genuine A-1 USED TRUCKS

A-1

USED CARS TRUCKS

Ford Dealers wanted both parts of the truck market back in the mid-fifties, old and new. So the earlier 1948-52 trucks were featured in "used" truck advertising. Clues, *October-November 1953*

During the late forties and early fifties, the Ford Motor Company liked to use insurance company statements to prove that its trucks lasted longer. The insurance companies used actuarial studies to prove their point. One must remember that these were the days before car manufacturers had survey companies to poll owners. These types of advertisement layout were used in newspapers. Ford Motor Company

them as an F-1, F-2 or F-3 model. The engine and chassis were identified by the same number, which gave the engine type, model series identification and consecutive unit number.

Ford gave the F-1 a 4,700 pound gross vehicle rating. The F-2 carried a 5,700 pound rating, and the F-3 came in at a whopping 6,800 pounds.

Back in 1948, Ford wanted to be your truck company—and it was serious about getting your business, as evidenced by its lineup. Buyers responded quite favorably to all these new Bonus Built Ford light commercial vehicles by buying more than 60,000 more vehicles in this range than in 1947. More than 143,000 Bonus Built light-duties rolled off the Ford assembly lines during 1948. This was a great year for Ford pickup truck sales, as more were sold than ever before. It was a good omen for this, the first, year for Ford's new postwar styling.

1949

"Built Stronger To Last Longer" was the catch phrase to describe the Ford truck lineup for model year 1949. In its second year the Bonus Built Ford trucks were changed just slightly, but for all practical purposes the vehicles were the same, so it's hard to tell the two apart. The chief changes were deleting the small red pinstripes from around the argent (silver) grille bars, and painting the wheels black instead of body color, as was done on the 1948 F-1. In addition, some trim pieces were painted instead of being chromed.

These pickups were billed as America's Lowest Priced Trucks, at an average base price of $1,300—buyers got a lot of truck for their money.

Two engines were offered again, the Rouge 226 and the Rouge 239 (Rouge designated that the engines were produced at Ford's engine plant in the Rouge complex in Dearborn, Michigan). Both engines were more than strong enough to meet any and all demands. They both featured a compression ratio of 6.8:1, allowing them to be run on regular fuel. Gross horsepower was again 100 at 3800 rpm for the V-8 and ninety-five at 3300 rpm for the six. Net horsepower figures with

Ford F-2 trucks were rated at three-quarter ton. These trucks had two-piece drive shafts and longer wheelbases, longer bodies and heavier-duty parts than the lighter-duty F-1s. Ford Motor Company

*BONUS: "Something given in addition to what is usual or strictly due"—Webster

EXTRA THRIFT! EXTRA RELIABILITY! EXTRA DURABILITY!

For a thrifty answer to fast delivery of light, bulky loads, choose the Bonus Built Ford Series F-2

IN THE SERIES F-2 YOU GET the lowest-priced 122-inch wheelbase truck in the Ford line.

You get a truck that handles a big 8-ft. Express body or a large 7½-ft. Platform or Stake. Costs are low, in the Ford tradition. This begins with low first-cost and carries on through exceptional gas, oil and maintenance economy for which Ford has always been noted.

Thrifty with costs, the F-2 gives outstanding performance. Loaded to rated capacity, it pulls up to a 9.5% smooth concrete grade in high gear.

The Ford F-2 offers a choice of either the 100-h.p. Ford V-8 or the 95-h.p. Ford Six. It features the Million Dollar Cab with insulated Level Action suspension. Full-floating rear axle with straddle-mounted pinion. 4-speed transmission. Heavy Duty 3-speed transmission also available. Airplane-type shock absorbers. And it's Bonus Built! Ford Series F-2 is built extra strong to last longer.

8-ft. Express; 7½-ft. Platform and Stake bodies available.

USING LATEST REGISTRATION DATA ON 6,106,000 TRUCKS, LIFE INSURANCE EXPERTS, WOLFE, CORCORAN AND LINDER OF NEW YORK CITY, PROVE FORD TRUCKS LAST LONGER!

FORD Division of FORD MOTOR COMPANY

This brochure is confusing because it shows a 1949 model and then states under "Trucks" that it's a 1959. "Built stronger to last longer." The two other pages give good specifications.

SERIES F-2 CHASSIS WITH CAB

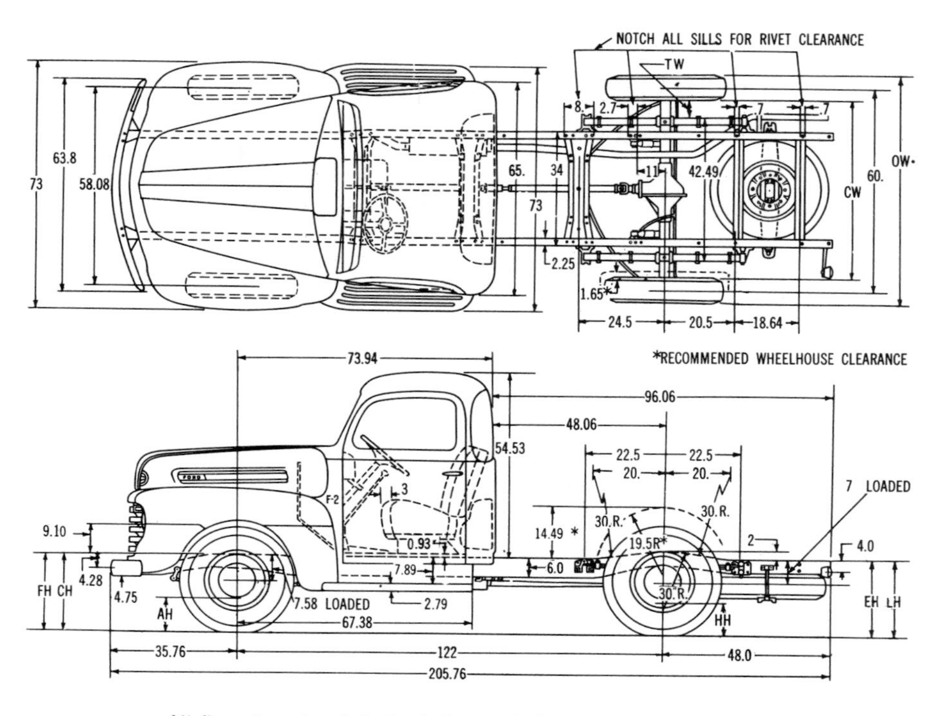

All dimensions given in inches (unless marked) and all weights are in pounds

FRONT VARIABLE DIMENSIONS

Front Tire Size	WIDTH		HEIGHT		
	Rim	Wheel Offset	FH Frame Height Light	CH Frame Height Loaded	AH Axle Clear-ance
6.50-16 6-p.r.	6L	0.56	21.39	20.98	8.37
7.00-16 6-p.r.	6L	0.56	22.29	21.88	9.27
7.50-16 6-p.r.	6L	0.56	22.69	22.28	9.67

P.r. denotes "ply rating." Front Spring Centers—29.0

CHASSIS WITH CAB WEIGHTS

CURB WEIGHT WITH TIRES SHOWN BELOW— FRONT, REAR AND SPARE			
Size	Front	Rear	Total
6.50-16 6-p.r.	2038	1218	3256
7.00-16 6-p.r.	2051	1237	3288
7.50-16 6-p.r.	2060	1250	3310

Curb weight is weight of empty vehicle ready to drive with fuel tank, cooling system and crankcase filled; tools, spare wheel, spare tire and all other equipment specified as standard. For dry weight—without fuel and water—deduct 160 lbs. from "total" weight.

REAR VARIABLE DIMENSIONS

Rear Tire Size	WIDTH						HEIGHT			
	Rim	Wheel Offset	Tire Section Dia.	CW Width Between Rear Tires	OW Width Over Rear Tires	TW Clearance Between Tire and Spring	Static Loaded Tire Radius	EH Frame Height Light	LH Frame Height Loaded	HH Axle Clearance
6.50-16 6-p.r.	6L	0.56	7.51	52.49	67.57	5.0	13.4	23.81	20.4	7.27
7.00-16 6-p.r.	6L	0.56	7.69	52.31	67.69	4.91	14.3	24.71	21.3	8.17
7.50-16 6-p.r.	6L	0.56	8.14	51.86	68.14	4.69	14.7	25.11	21.7	8.57

P.r. denotes "ply rating." Rear Spring Centers—40.25

Recommended Body Length (Inside)	
Nominal (Feet)	Range (Feet)
7½	7—8

SERIES F-2 CHASSIS SPECIFICATIONS

MAXIMUM GROSS VEHICLE WEIGHT 5,700 POUNDS

AXLE, FRONT

Capacity-lbs.......2500
Type.......Reverse Elliott Modified I-Beam
Material.......Heat-Treated Alloy Steel Forging
Size (Height x Width x Web)—in.......2.29 x 1.6 x 0.25
Thrust Bearing.......Tapered Roller or Anti-Friction Ball
Wheel Bearings.....High Capacity, Dual Opposed, Adjustable Tapered Roller
Tie Rod......Ball Stud and Socket, Spring Loaded for Automatic Take-up of Wear, Equipped with Rubber Dust Shields

AXLE, REAR

Capacity—lbs.......4000
Type.......Spiral Bevel—Full Floating
Housing—Center—Type.......Split
Pinion—Mounting—Drive End Type.......Straddle—S.A.E. Taper
Ring Gear Thrust Plate.......Fixed Shoe
Differential.......4-Pinion
Side and Pinion Gear Thrust Washers.......Steel
Pinion Shaft Front Bearing.......Dual Opposed Tapered Roller
Pinion Shaft Rear Bearing.......Straight Roller
Differential Side Bearings.......Tapered Roller
Axle Shaft Material.......Forged, Special Manganese Steel
Axle Shaft Diameter at Spline—in.......1.37
Wheel Bearings.......Dual Opposed Tapered Roller
Number Wedge-type Driving Dowels—Each Hub.......8
Lubricant Capacity—pints.......3
Axle Ratio—Standard.......4.86 to 1

BRAKES, SERVICE

Type.......Hydraulic, Two-Shoe, Double Anchor, Self-Centering
Front Brake (Drum Diam. x Lining Width—Thickness)—in......12 x 1¾—3/16
Rear Brake (Drum Diam. x Lining Width—Thickness)—in......12 x 1¾—3/16
Total Drum Area—sq. in.......264
Total Lining Area—sq. in.......167
Drums—Type.......Demountable
Material.......Composite—Cast Iron Fused to Steel Back

BRAKE, HAND.......Cable with Equalizer Applying Rear Wheel Brakes

BUMPER

Type.......Curved, Truck-Type Channel
Mounting.......Bolted Direct to Front of Frame Side Rails

CLUTCH

Type.......Gyro-Grip, Semi-Centrifugal Single Plate
Diameter, Outside—in.......11
Total Frictional Area—sq. in.......123.7
Cover Plate.......Ventilated Type
Pressure Plate.......Cast Iron
Clutch Disc.......Cushioned Hub with Vibration Damper
Release Bearing.......Sealed Ball, Pre-lubricated
Pilot Bearing.......Copper Graphite Bushing
Attachment—Levers to Pressure Plate.......Needle Roller Bearings
Clutch Plate Pressure, lbs.: at Zero Speed—at 3000 RPM.......1044—1439
Pedal Pressure, lbs.: at Zero Speed—at 3000 RPM.......34—45

COOLING SYSTEM

Capacity—qts.: Six.......18
V-8.......23
Radiator.......Flat Tube and Fin—Pressure Cap
Thermostat(s).......In Engine Water Outlet(s)
Fan, Diameter—in.: Six.......17—4-Blade
V-8.......18½—4-Blade

DRIVE LINE

Type.......Hotchkiss, Straight-Line Drive
Propeller Shafts—Number.......Two, Tubular, Forged Steel Ends
Diameter, in.......2.0
Universal Joints—Number, type.......Three, Needle Roller Bearing
Center Bearing.......Rubber Encased Ball Type

ELECTRICAL SYSTEM

Battery.......6-Volt, 15-Plate, 90-Amp. Hr. Capacity
Generator.......35 Amp., 250 Watts, Air Cooled, Shunt Wound, External Voltage and Current Regulated
Ignition.......Loadomatic Vacuum Controlled System, Fully Automatic Distributor; Metal-Clad Coil; Open Wiring in Rubber Grommets
Head Lights.......Sealed Beam, Foot-Switch Beam Control
Starter.......High Torque, Automatic Engagement, Solenoid Switch, Push Button Control
Parking Lights; Left-hand Combination Stop and Tail Light; Instrument Lights; Ignition Switch with Key Lock; Circuit Breakers; Voltage Regulator.

ENGINES

	Truck Six	*Truck V-8*
No. Cylinders—Bore and Stroke, in.	6—3.3 x 4.4	8—3³⁄₁₆ x 3¾
Displacement—cu. in.	226	239
Taxable HP rating (N.A.C.C.)	26.1	32.5
Max. Brake Horsepower—RPM	95 @ 3300	100 @ 3800
Max. Torque—Lbs.-Ft.—RPM	180 @ 1200	180 @ 2000
Compression Ratio	6.8 to 1	6.8 to 1

FRAME

Side Rail—Type.......Tapered Channel Section
Max. Section (Depth x Flange x Thick.)—in......6.0 x 2.25 x 0.19
Cross Members.......6—Flanged "U" Type and Channel Section
Section Modulus.......3.34

FUEL SYSTEM

Carburetor.......Downdraft
Air Cleaner.......Heavy Duty Oil Bath, One Qt. Capacity
Fuel Pump and Filter.......Diaphragm Type, Driven from Camshaft
Fuel Tank—Chassis without Cab.......17-Gal. Inside Left Frame Rail
Chassis with Cab.......20-Gal. Back of Seat
Fuel Filler.......Tube Extension to Outside Cab or Body

LUBRICATION

Engine.......Full Pressure Feed to all Main, Crankpin and Camshaft Bearings
Oil Filter.......Replaceable Cartridge Type
Oil Pan.......Clean-out Plate in Bottom of Pan
Crankcase Capacity.......6 Qts. (dry); 5 Qts. (refill)
Chassis.......Fittings for Pressure Lubrication

SHOCK ABSORBERS

Front and Rear.......Direct, Double Acting, Permanently Sealed, Telescopic

SPRINGS—Semi-Elliptic, Ford Alloy Steel

	Front	*Rear*
Length x Width—in.	36 x 1.75	45 x 2.25
Number of Leaves and Defl. Rate—lbs. per in.	8—423	12—465
Capacity (at Normal Deflection)—Per Spring, lbs.	1025	1950

STEERING

Type.......Worm and Single Row Needle Bearing Roller
Ratio.......18.2 to 1
Wheel.......18 in. Dia., 3-Spoke
Turning Radius—ft.......22 (Right); 23 (Left)

TRANSMISSION

Type.......4-Speed, Selective Sliding Spur Gear
Lubricant Capacity—pints.......5

Gear Positions	*First*	*Second*	*Third*	*High*	*Reverse*
Ratio (to 1)	6.40	3.09	1.69	1.00	7.83

Power Take-Off Opening.......S.A.E. 6-Bolt, on Right Side

WHEELS AND TIRES

Wheels.......5—16-inch Steel Disc with 0.56-inch Offset; 8 Hole, 6.5-inch Dia. Bolt Circle
Rims—Size and Type.......16 x 6L, Drop Center
Tires—Standard Size—Front, Rear and Spare.......6.50-16 6-ply rating

CHASSIS EQUIPMENT, included as standard, in addition to items specified above:

Hood, Cowl and Dash Assembly
Front Fenders
Center Cowl Ventilator
Steel Toe Boards
Instrument Panel
Speedometer with Odometer
Water Temperature Gage
Fuel Gage
Oil Pressure Gage
Charge Indicator
Ash Receptacle
Dispatch Box
Choke Button
Light Switch
Left-hand Windshield Wiper (except chassis-cowl)
Treadle Type Accelerator Pedal
Spare Wheel and Tire
Spare Tire Carrier Under Frame
Single Electric Horn
Front and Rear License Brackets
Mechanical Jack (1½ Ton Capacity)
Standard Tools in Tool Bag, including Pliers; Screw Driver; Tire Iron; Rear Wheel Bearing Nut Wrench; Spark Plug and Cylinder Head Bolt Wrench; Wheel Stud Nut Wrench; Jack Handle; Tire Carrier Wrench.

NOTE: Running boards are not standard on chassis with cowl or windshield. Hub caps are available as an Accessory only.

OPTIONAL EQUIPMENT (Installed in Production) includes—

Heavy Duty 3-Speed Transmission
Tires; Front, Rear and Spare—
7.00-16 6-ply rating
7.50-16 6-ply rating
Sponge Rubber Pad in Seat (Cab)
Spiralounge Driver's Seat (Cab)
Heater and Defroster—
Recirculating Type†
Fresh Air Intake Type†
Heavy Duty Radiator
Heavy Duty Fan
Right-hand Tail Light
Right-hand Windshield Wiper*†

*In areas required by law only. †Except chassis-cowl.

FINISH AND COLOR COMBINATIONS

(Items starred (*) are not applicable to chassis with cowl or windshield)

Frame, Bumper, Wheels, Running Boards*, Rear View Mirror*, Vent Window Frame*, 17-gal. Frame-mounted Fuel Tank, Filler Neck and Cap, Tail Lamp.......Black
Grille Recess and Grille Bars.......M1733 Aluminum
Hood Moldings, Windshield Wiper (except cowl), Door Handles*, Head and Parking Lamp Doors, Name and Identification Plates.......Bright Finish
Fenders, Hood, Cowl, Cab, (including all interior metal surfaces before trimming) and Bodies.......Body Color▲

Body Color Options

M1722 Vermilion
M1724 Medium Luster Black
M14283 Meadow Green
M14286 Birch Gray
M14301 Chrome Yellow

▲Cowl and Cowl-Windshield models are finished in prime coat only unless body color is specified.

THE FORD MOTOR COMPANY, WHOSE POLICY IS ONE OF CONTINUOUS IMPROVEMENT, RESERVES THE RIGHT TO CHANGE AT ANY TIME, SPECIFICATIONS, DESIGN OR PRICES WITHOUT INCURRING OBLIGATION.

accessories installed showed ninety for the V-8 and eighty-seven for the six, quite respectable.

Also, both engines offered lots of torque, at low rpm for their sizes, providing plenty of reserve pulling power and economy. Peak torque was reached by both engines at a relatively low rpm reading of 1200, with the six pegged at 178 pounds-feet and the V-8 at 180.

Transmission choices were limited to manual boxes, including a regular three-speed column shift and two optional floor-mounted versions: a four-speed and a heavy-duty three-speed.

Once again Ford offered the F-1 half-ton, the F-2 three-quarter-ton and the F-3 three-quarter-ton heavy-duty. Curb weights ranged from a low of approximately 3,000 pounds for the F-1 pickup with a 6½ foot box to a high of 3,700 pounds for the F-3 with an eight-foot express body.

If the F-1 was the lightweight, the F-2 had to be considered the middleweight, and the F-3, the heavyweight. Though it carried a one-quarter-ton-lower rating than the old Ford Tonner, the F-3 was designed to do the work of the heavier unit. Everything about the F-3s said "heavy-duty" and Ford advertised them as the "little giants of trucking." That claim wasn't too far-fetched; most of the parts found in the F-3 saw duty in the larger series. Though they shared most of the F-2 components and looked similar, at least on the surface, there was much more truck found under the F-3 skin. For the F-3, Ford specified larger wheels (seventeen inch) and better tires, along with bigger brakes and larger clutches, axles, springs and shocks. These were tough trucks that saw many years of

1950.

Interior details of a 1950 F-1 standard cab.

dependable service. Some of them are still running and hauling the way they did way back when.

All Ford light commercial vehicles came with an impressive array of standard features. Some of these features were either extra-cost or items not offered on other makes. They included a center cowl ventilation panel and a full instrument panel with speedometer, odometer, water temperature gauge, fuel gauge, ammeter and oil temperature gauge. There were also an electric horn, spare wheel and tire with frame-mounted carrier, tool kit, jack, ashtray, choke button and a host of others. For the owner with more money, Ford offered an optional equipment list that was almost as long as the standard list.

Though these vehicles were meant for commercial purposes, Ford went to great pains to make sure they didn't look bland. Five bright exterior color choices were offered: Vermilion (bright red), Meadow Green, Black, Birch Gray and Chrome Yellow. The same colors were offered in 1948. These were the standard colors; other colors were available for special orders, including just a bare prime coat. The frame, bumper, running boards, rearview mirror, window frames, gas filler neck and gas cap were all painted black. An aluminum (argent) finish was placed on the grille bars and recessed grille backboard. On the interior, all metal areas were finished in body color. The wheels could be black or body color. On the panel vans, the running boards were finished in body color.

In 1949, Ford offered a total of thirty-eight different models in the light-duty category, and once again it offered something for everybody, a fact that was not lost in the marketplace. Ford trucks were quite popular that year, and the pickups were the stars that shined the brightest. Ford released them in December 1948, and over 138,000 of them were produced. That amount was down slightly from the previous year but, with everything considered, it wasn't too bad.

1950

On January 20, 1950, the 1950 Ford trucks were unveiled to the public, and once again there was hardly any difference from the year before. A minor running change was moving the shift lever from the floor to the

Radio block-off plate, circa 1950.

Here is a 1950 F-1 standard cab showing cowl ventilator assembly in the open position. Note one windshield wiper and no brightwork around windshield.

steering column on the standard three-speed F-1. This change offered more room and comfort in the cab—it allowed three adults to sit in the cab without one having to straddle the shift lever.

Over in the car ranks, Ford claimed there were fifty new items found on the 1950 models, but in the truck line it was more of the same. Once again, the 1950 series lineup included the F-1, F-2 and F-3, with thirty-eight models featuring the same equipment, almost the same colors (Sheridan Blue, Palisade Green and Silvertone Grey added), the same ratings and so on. Prices ranged from a low of $960 for a cowl-and-chassis (six) model to a high of $1,575 for an F-3 stake (V-8).

Though everything was the same this year, the Ford light commercial vehicles sold over 234,000 units, a new sales record. That was up almost 100,000 vehicles from the previous year's sales. I don't think this increase happened because of anything Ford did, but because of two events outside the company. One, the Chrysler Company faced a strike that lasted about three months; without the Dodge pickup among the competition Ford had less to worry about. Two, the United States entered the Korean War. Many people feared that the assembly lines would be shut down again, so they bought new vehicles while they were still available. Ford was happy about the outcome, but knew it

Interior detail shot, 1950 Ford F-1 driver's door. Its all-metal construction seems rather stark today, but back in the early fifties trucks were meant to be functional, and niceties were kept to a minimum. Ribs were punched into the metal to add support and to make a more stable mounting source for bolting on the door and window-cranking mechanisms. Removal panel at bottom was designed for easy access to the window crank and door-opening mechanisms.

Left door of a 1950 Ford F-1. Note windwing window, hinge-mounted mirror and door handle.

wouldn't last and had already decided to alter the 1951 offerings.

Because of the Chrysler strike, Ford moved into second place in the manufacturers standings, and hasn't looked back. Perhaps that might not have happened, had Ford not changed some things back in 1945.

1951

If 1950 was the year for "fifty ways new" for the Ford cars, then 1951 was the year for "fifty-one ways new" for the Ford trucks. Though similar in size, shape and appearance to the earlier models, Ford's 1951 Bonus Built trucks were updated in many details.

The front fenders and grille cavity were extensively changed to provide for a new, wider grille. Instead of using five thin horizontal bars, the new models featured one large horizontal bar that was supplemented by vertical posts topped by a curious sphere arrangement. When production started, these grilles were painted argent (silver) to complement the chrome-plated headlight rings. However, during production, the Defense Department issued an edict curtailing the use of some of the metals used in the chroming process. So the grille bars on these trucks were painted an ivory color and the headlight rings were painted argent.

Parking lights were moved under the headlights and the recessed grille panel board was deleted because the headlights were freestanding. Also up front was a newly designed, frame-mounted bumper.

Moving to the hood area, one found quite a few changes. The bull-nose molding was changed somewhat to allow a new front vent system. New brightwork surrounded the vent. The Ford name was carried on this piece of trim, instead of single letters pre-

1950 F-1 front-end details. Note two-piece fender and vent on hood front, ivory-colored grille cavity and horizontal grille bars.

GMC and Chevrolet used the same bodies, except for trim differences, from the late forties through the early fifties. These GM trucks looked as clean as their Ford counterparts. These early GM trucks (a 1950 shown here) seem to be favored more than their 1955-56 counterparts by truck enthusiasts. The exact opposite is true with Ford truck fanciers.

viously carried on the upper grille support panel. The hood also carried new side vents and new trim. On the upper grille support, a chromed V-8 emblem was used on those trucks so equipped. On the new Five Star Extra (deluxe) cabs, the windshield molding was chromed.

In back, the pickup bed and tailgate were redesigned for easier loading. The side panels and corner supports were changed slightly to provide more carrying space. The bed had a floor made of hardwood planks held together by metal strips, instead of the all-metal floor that was used before. The rear window was fifty percent larger, making it easier to see around and outside the cab.

Left-hand door of 1950 F-1. Note F-1 plate, hinge-mounted mirror and vent window.

On the inside, buyers had a choice of two trim levels. The standard offering was called the Five Star. With it, buyers got a three-way air control unit with air wing ventilators and a cowl panel that also acted as a ventilator. They also got a tough vinyl seat covering over rubberized hair padding (a composite material of horsehair and bonded rubber) and coil springs; an adjustable driver's-side visor; dual windshield wipers; an easy-to-read, fully gauged instrument cluster; a dispatch (glove) box; an ashtray; and an adjustable seat. Some of these standard items weren't even offered as options on the competition.

The second trim level offering was called the Five Star Extra. Buyers of this version were given all the standard options plus dual electric horns instead of a single horn, foam-rubber seat padding, two-tone seat upholstery (vinyl and mohair), deluxe door trim panels and a sound-deadening headliner that

Detail of 1950 F-1 right-hand door, showing back of cab sculpturing, gas filler and door handle.

covered a fiberglass pad. Other sound-deadening devices were used throughout the cab. The Extra also used special door panel trim, bright window trim, door locks, armrests, cigarette lighter and domelight with automatic door-control switches. All this extra equipment was designed to ease some of the driver's burdens. With all that going for it, the Five Star Extra was just about the classiest cab found in the low-priced field.

Ford also made some changes in the power department, although it didn't need to because most manufacturers at that time offered only one engine, not two. But Ford figured if some changes were good, more were better—and the better its trucks were, the more the company hoped to sell.

Ford called its power changes Step Ahead Engineering and started out with new piston ring designs. The top ring was chromed to provide for better oil control and to reduce oil consumption. Chrome plating helped to make them tougher, thus extending their lives and reducing maintenance costs—important considerations to truck buyers at that time.

Also new were free-turning valves that offered a self-cleaning feature. Controlling these new valves was a newly designed high-lift camshaft that offered more power potential. A new aluminum alloy was used in piston

Left front sheet metal on a 1950 F-1. Note hood trim and two-piece front fender. The whitewalls were a stock option, though seldom seen when the trucks were new.

This fine example of a 1950 F-1 belongs to Bob Fortin of Massachusetts.

The stock 239 ci Flattie is under the hood of this 1950 owned by Fred Martin of Massachusetts.

Fred Martin of Massachusetts owns this restored 1950 F-1.

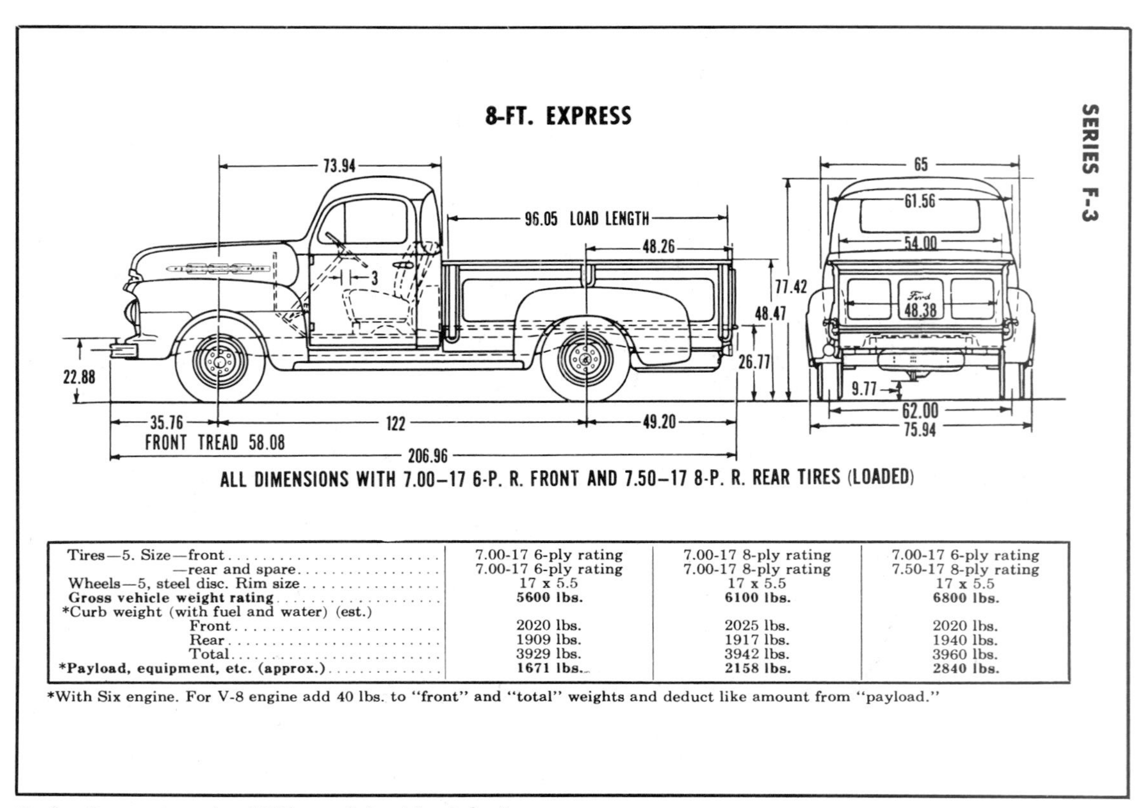

Tires—5. Size—front	7.00-17 6-ply rating	7.00-17 8-ply rating	7.00-17 6-ply rating
—rear and spare	7.00-17 6-ply rating	7.00-17 8-ply rating	7.50-17 8-ply rating
Wheels—5, steel disc. Rim size	17 x 5.5	17 x 5.5	17 x 5.5
Gross vehicle weight rating	**5600 lbs.**	**6100 lbs.**	**6800 lbs.**
*Curb weight (with fuel and water) (est.)			
Front	2020 lbs.	2025 lbs.	2020 lbs.
Rear	1909 lbs.	1917 lbs.	1940 lbs.
Total	3929 lbs.	3942 lbs.	3960 lbs.
***Payload, equipment, etc. (approx.)**	**1671 lbs.**	**2158 lbs.**	**2840 lbs.**

*With Six engine. For V-8 engine add 40 lbs. to "front" and "total" weights and deduct like amount from "payload."

Body dimensions for 1951 model with eight-foot truck bed.

Panel van brochure for 1951 shows airbrush artist's work at its best. Delivery driver seems undersize!

FORD SERIES F-1

SERIES F-1, 6½-FT. PICKUP

MAX. G.V.W., 4700 LBS. Wheelbase: 114 inches

Payloads range up to 1480 lbs.! New body has sturdy interlocked, straight-grained wood floor protected by steel skid strips. Floor and skid strips extend fully to the box end and are flush with lowered tailgate to furnish an all-level platform for sliding heavy crates easily, from tailgate into body. This, plus very low loading height of 24", gives the man who loads it a "big break." All-welded steel body construction and snug-fitting tailgate produce a rigid body that's grain-tight. High 20-inch side panels give more protection against load shifting. Rolled tailgate edge tapers to maximum size at center to prevent sag under heavy loads. This economical F-1 Pickup is the most popular truck in the Ford line!

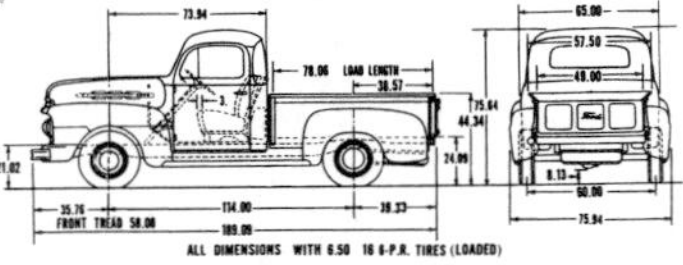

SERIES F-1, 8-FT. PANEL

MAX. G.V.W., 4700 LBS. Wheelbase: 114 inches

This handsome F-1 Panel takes payloads up to 1330 lbs. in a welded, all-steel body sealed against dust, fumes and weather. The sturdy steel frame is reinforced with brackets for even longer life. Full width is 5' and extra length alongside the driver's seat accommodates loads up to 11½' long! The solid plywood floor is stoutly reinforced and protected by steel skid strips to reduce wear. Sealing of floor to body side panels and tight, rubber rear door seals effectively exclude dust, fumes and moisture from merchandise and driver. Heavy door checks let rear doors open fully or hold them firmly at 90° opening for quick loading and unloading. For the smartest truck on the road, choose the 5-STAR EXTRA Panel which gives you many additional features for top riding ease, driver efficiency and load protection at slight extra cost.

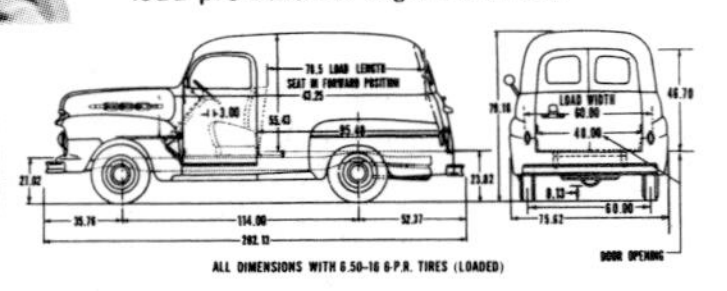

SERIES F-1, 6½-FT. PLATFORM STAKE

MAX. G.V.W., 4700 LBS. Wheelbase: 114 inches

You can pile the loads sky-high on this Ford F-1 Platform-Stake! The loads can be weighty, too . . . up to 1530 lbs.! The well-seasoned, sturdy wood floor is permanently protected by steel skid strips that aid in loading and unloading bulky cargoes. One-piece side and end stake racks are fashioned of sturdy, straight-grained wood. They are quickly, easily removed to facilitate loading, and are locked in place by firm-gripping steel interlocking plates bolted to the racks. A heavy steel rub rail and steel caps on body sill ends offer platform protection all around, when backing into or parking alongside loading docks. The F-1 Platform Stake offers famous Ford Truck value in its low initial and operating costs, plus ease of maintenance and low-cost parts replacement.

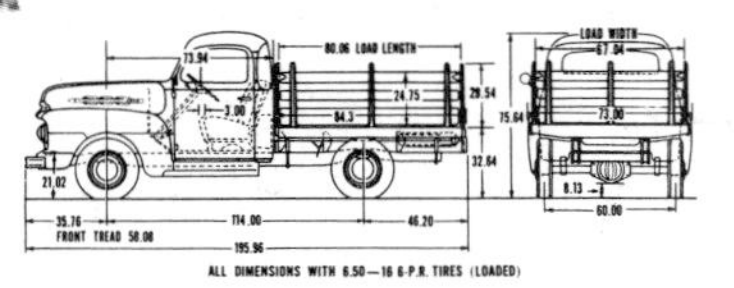

Series F-1 Color Options: VERMILION, MEADOW GREEN, SEA ISLAND GREEN, RAVEN BLACK, SILVERTONE GRAY, SHERIDAN BLUE, ALPINE BLUE

Body style comparisons in the official 1951 brochure. Again, the airbrush artist has distorted relative dimensions. Real-life trucks are more handsome.

construction that allowed for expansion as the pistons got hot. This feature increased power and improved cylinder sealing. Even the main and rod bearings were redesigned. New water pumps helped the engines run cooler, and the ignition system was touted as being waterproof.

Power with economy was the emphasis in 1951 Ford truck advertising. It was stated that Ford's new Step Ahead Engineering achieved new levels of economic operation. One of the chief reasons for this accomplishment was Ford's new Power Pilot system, a vacuum-advance mechanism that tied the distributor into the fuel-metering system. This system allowed fuel metering, depending on load conditions; it automatically adjusted the spark to meet changing requirements. In this manner, spark knock was virtually eliminated and an owner/driver could gain more economy of operation by using lower-cost regular fuels. Compared to all the gadgetry we have today, the system sounds simple, but in 1951 it was considered a revolutionary improvement.

This year the clutches were smaller and the brakes were larger. The new clutches offered easier engagement while the new brakes offered more stopping power. There were also revisions made to the steering system and to the new airplane-type shocks.

Not all of the changes were of a functional nature; some were strictly cosmetic, like the improved exterior color selections. Joining the old favorites of red, black, green, gray and yellow were Sea Island Green and Alpine Blue.

Even with these changes, the price structure stayed pretty close to previous levels, so 1951 Ford truck buyers got even more truck value for their dollar. The market responded favorably to these new changes, as Ford sold 188,000 units during the model year. And that was pretty good considering that it was a four-year-old design. Though not new, there

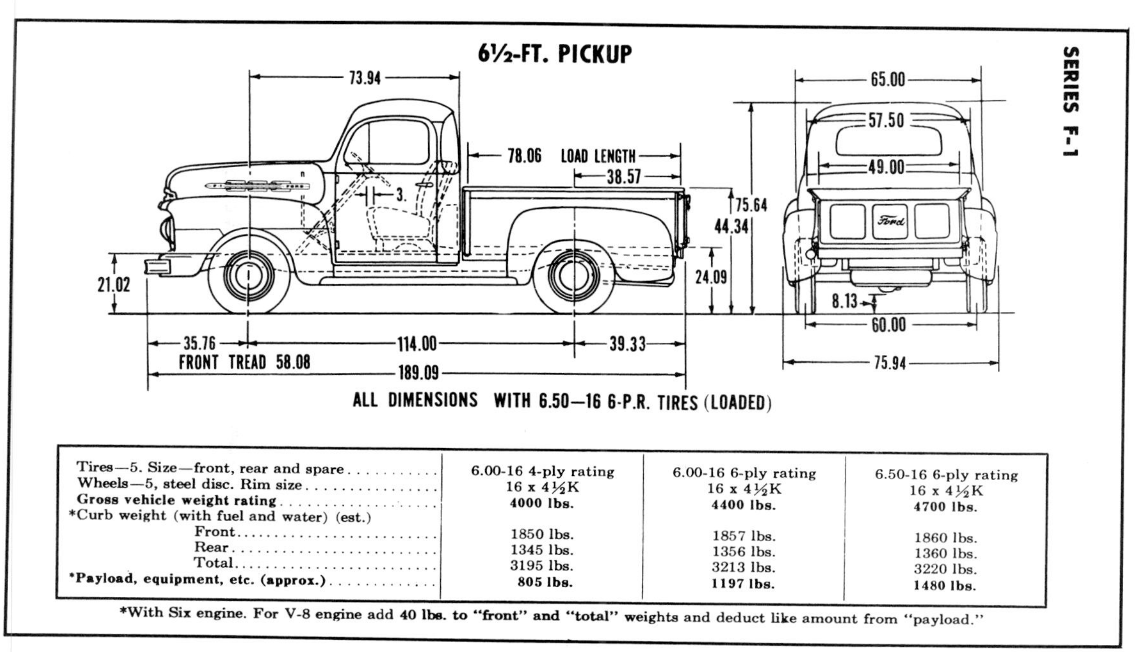

Tires—5. Size—front, rear and spare	6.00-16 4-ply rating	6.00-16 6-ply rating	6.50-16 6-ply rating
Wheels—5, steel disc. Rim size	16 x 4½K	16 x 4½K	16 x 4½K
Gross vehicle weight rating	**4000 lbs.**	**4400 lbs.**	**4700 lbs.**
*Curb weight (with fuel and water) (est.)			
Front	1850 lbs.	1857 lbs.	1860 lbs.
Rear	1345 lbs.	1356 lbs.	1360 lbs.
Total	3195 lbs.	3213 lbs.	3220 lbs.
***Payload, equipment, etc. (approx.)**	**805 lbs.**	**1197 lbs.**	**1480 lbs.**

*With Six engine. For V-8 engine add 40 lbs. to "front" and "total" weights and deduct like amount from "payload."

Light-duty models pocket specifications—one page looks like this.

SERIES F-1 SPECIFICATIONS

MAXIMUM GROSS VEHICLE WEIGHT 4,700 POUNDS

AXLE, FRONT

Capacity—lbs.	2500
Type	Modified I-Beam
Material	Heat-treated Alloy Steel Forging
Size (Height x Width x Web)—in.	2.29 x 1.6 x 0.25

AXLE, REAR

Capacity—lbs.	3000
Type	Hypoid—Semi-Floating
Housing	Integral—Tubes Pressed-in and Welded to Carrier Casting
Pinion—Mounting—Drive End Type	Overhung—10-Spline
Differential	2-Pinion
Axle Shaft Diameter at Spline—in.	1.25
Axle Ratio—Standard	3.92 to 1
Optional	4.27 to 1

BRAKES, SERVICE

Type	Hydraulic, Two-Shoe, Single Anchor, Self-Energizing
Front Brake (Drum Diam. x Lining Width—Thickness)—in.	11 x 2—3/16
Rear Brake (Drum Diam. x Lining Width—Thickness)—in.	11 x 1¾—3/16
Total Drum Area—sq. in.	259
Total Lining Area—sq. in.	178
Drums—Type	Demountable
Material	Composite—Cast Iron Fused to Steel Back

BRAKE, HAND .... Cable with Equalizer applying Rear Wheel Brakes

BUMPER

Type	Curved, Truck-Type Channel
Mounting	Bolted Direct to Front of Frame Side Rails

CLUTCH

Type	Gyro-Grip, Semi-Centrifugal Single Plate
Diameter, Outside—in.	10
Total Frictional Area—sq. in.	85.5
Cover Plate	Ventilated Type
Pressure Plate	Cast Iron
Clutch Disc	Cushioned Hub with Vibration Damper
Release Bearing	Sealed Ball, Pre-lubricated
Pilot Bearing	Copper Graphite Bushing
Attachment—Levers to Pressure Plate	Needle Roller Bearings
Clutch Plate Pressure, lbs.: at Zero Speed—at 3000 RPM	1089—1669
Pedal Pressure, lbs.: at Zero Speed—at 3000 RPM	32—40

COOLING SYSTEM

Capacity—qts.: Six	17
V-8	23
Radiator	Flat Tube and Fin—Pressure Cap
Thermostat(s)	In Engine Water Outlet(s)
Fan, Diameter—in.: Six	17—4-Blade
V-8	18½—4-Blade

DRIVE LINE

Type	Hotchkiss, Straight-Line Drive
Propeller Shaft—Number	One, Tubular, Forged Steel Ends
Diameter, in.	3.5
Universal Joints—Number, Type	Two, Needle Roller Bearing

ELECTRICAL SYSTEM

Battery— 95-H.P. Six	6-Volt, 17-Plate, 100-Amp. Hr. Capacity
100-H.P. V-8	6-Volt, 15-Plate, 90-Amp. Hr. Capacity
Generator	35 Amp., 250 Watts
Ignition	Full Vacuum Controlled System Fully Automatic Distributor; Metal-Clad Coil; Open Wiring in Rubber Grommets with Moisture-Proof Boots Over Spark Plugs
Head Lights	Sealed Beam, Foot-Switch Beam Control
Starter	High Torque, Automatic Engagement, Solenoid Switch, Push Button Control

Parking Lights; Left-hand Combination Stop and Tail Light (Dual Tail Lights standard on Panel); Instrument Lights; Ignition Switch with Key Lock; Circuit Breakers; Voltage Regulator.

ENGINES

	TRUCK SIX	TRUCK V-8
No. Cylinders—Bore and Stroke, in.	6—3.3 x 4.4	8—3 3/16 x 3¾
Displacement—cu. in.	226	239
Max. Brake Horsepower@RPM	95 @ 3300	100 @ 3800
Max. Torque—Lbs.-Ft.@RPM	180 @ 1200	180 @ 2000
Compression Ratio	6.8 to 1	6.8 to 1

FRAME

Side Rail—Type	Tapered Channel Section
Max. Section (Depth x Flange x Thick.) in.	5.92 x 2.25 x 0.15
Cross Members	4—Flanged "U" Type and Channel Section
Section Modulus	2.65

FUEL SYSTEM

Carburetor	Downdraft
Air Cleaner	Heavy Duty Oil Bath, One Qt. Capacity
Fuel Pump and Filter	Diaphragm Type, Driven from Camshaft
Fuel Tank—Chassis without Cab	17-Gal. Inside Left Frame Rail
Chassis with Cab	20-Gal. Back of Seat
Fuel Filler	Tube Extension to Outside Cab or Body

LUBRICATON

Engine	Full Pressure Feed to all Main, Crankpin and Camshaft Bearings
Oil Pan	Clean-out Plate in Bottom of Pan
Crankcase Capacity (with opt. oil filter)	6 qts. (dry); 5 qts. (refill)
Chassis	Fittings for Pressure Lubrication

SHOCK ABSORBERS

Front and Rear	Direct, Double Acting, Permanently Sealed, Telescopic

SPRINGS—Semi-Elliptic, Ford Alloy Steel

	FRONT	REAR
Length x Width—in.	36 x 1¾	45 x 2
Number of Leaves and Defl. Rate—lbs. per in.	8—243	10—275*
Capacity (at Normal Deflection)—Per Spring	850	1350*

*Panels Only—9 Leaves, Rate 230 lbs. per in., Capacity 1050 lbs.

STEERING

Type	Worm and Single Row Needle Bearing Roller
Ratio	18.2 to 1
Wheel	18 In. Dia., 3-Spoke
Turning Radius—ft.	21¼ (right); 22½ (left)
Tie Rod	Ball Stud and Socket, Spring Loaded for Automatic Take-up of Wear, Equipped with Rubber Dust Shields

TRANSMISSION

Type .... 3-Speed, All-Helical, Synchronizers 2nd and High with Steering Column Gearshift Lever

Gear Positions	FIRST	SECOND	HIGH	REVERSE
Ratio (to 1)	2.78	1.62	1.000	3.63

WHEELS AND TIRES

Wheels	5—16-inch Steel Disc with 0.62-inch Offset; 5 Hole, 5.5-inch Dia. Bolt Circle
Rims—Size and Type	16 x 4½K, Drop Center
Tires—Standard Size—Front, Rear and Spare	6.00-16 4-ply rating

CHASSIS EQUIPMENT, included as standard, in addition to items specified above:

Hood, Cowl and Dash Assembly
Front Fenders
Center Cowl Ventilator
Steel Toe Boards
Instrument Panel
Speedometer with Odometer
Water Temperature Gage
Oil Pressure Gage
Fuel Gage
Charge Indicator
Ash Receptacle
Dispatch Box
Choke Button
Light Switch
Treadle Type Accelerator Pedal
Bright Hub Caps, Front and Rear
Dual Windshield Wipers (except Cowl)
Single Electric Horn
Spare Tire Carrier
Air Wing Ventilating Windows in Doors
Fenders, Rear—on Pickup and Panels (Splash Guards on Stake and Platform)
Mirror, Rear View—
Inside on Pickup
Left, Outside, Short Arm on Panels
Left, Outside, Long Arm on Chassis-Cab, Stake & Platform
Running Boards—
Long (curved at rear end for fender) on Pickup
Long (straight at rear end) on Chassis-Cab
Short on Panels, Stake and Platform
Rear Bumper (Panels only)
Sun Visor—Left side in Cab
Mechanical Jack (1½ ton Capacity)
Standard Tools in tool bag including: pliers; screw driver; tire iron; spark plug and cylinder head bolt wrench; wheel stud nut wrench; jack handle.

NOTE: Running boards are not standard on chassis with cowl or windshield.

AVAILABLE EQUIPMENT (Installed in Production) includes—

Oil Filter, Replaceable Cartridge Type
4.27 to 1 Axle Ratio
Tires: Front, Rear and Spare
6.00-16 6-ply rating
6.50-16 6-ply rating
11" Clutch with Std. 3-Speed Transmission
H.D. 3-Spd. Transmission with 11" Clutch and Floor Gearshift
4-Spd. Transmission with 11" Clutch and Floor Gearshift
5-STAR EXTRA Cab complete, including Distinctive Chassis Trim
5-STAR EXTRA Panel, including Distinctive Chassis Trim.
Auxiliary Seat for F-1 Panel. Auxiliary Seat with Two-Tone Upholstery for 5-STAR EXTRA Panel.
Heater and Defroster*—
Recirculating Type
Fresh Air Intake Type
*Except Chassis-Cowl
Electric Windshield Wipers (Six)
Combination Fuel and Vacuum Booster Pump for positive Windshield Wiper Action (V-8)
Heavy Duty Radiator
Rear Bumper (for Pickup, Chassis-Cab, -Cowl, and -Windshield)
Heavy Duty Fan
Right Hand Tail Light (Note: Std. on Panels)

SERIES F-1 BODY SPECIFICATIONS—CONDENSED

6½-FT. PICKUP BODY	**BODY**—welded steel construction. **CORNER POSTS**—Box type, welded to body. **FLARES**—reinforced rolled top.	**FLOOR**—sturdy wood protected by steel skid strips. **FRONT PANEL**—full height, reinforced.	**LOAD SPACE**—78.06" long; 49" wide; 20" to top of flare; 45 cu. ft. capacity. **LOADING HEIGHT**—24", floor to ground.	**STAKE POCKETS**—four, in corner posts. **TAILGATE**—stamped panel design; reinforced edge; anti-rattle chains.
8-FT. PANEL BODY	**BODY**—reinforced welded steel; top and side panels shaped and welded to rear fenders. **DRIVER'S COMPARTMENT**—spacious; weather-sealed windows, doors. Individual type driver's seat, 3" adjustment. 5-STAR EXTRA Panel has many features for added riding ease, style and driver efficiency.	**FLOOR**—solid plywood, well supported. Dust-, moisture-sealed at body side panels. **INTERIOR**—steel panel-protected sides, floor to top of wheelhouses—Panel has wood slats above; 5-STAR EXTRA Panel has heavy masonite lining above and perforated headlining on roof panel, backed by thick glass wool insulating pad.	**LOAD SPACE**—95.4" long on floor (138.5" alongside driver); 60" wide; 55.43" high. Total capacity (including space beside driver) 160.3 cu. ft. **LOADING HEIGHT**—23.82", floor to ground.	**LOCKS**—rear panel doors and right hand (Panel), right and left hand (5-STAR EXTRA Panel). **REAR DOORS**—hinged to welded one-piece steel door frame; fitted with soft rubber seals. 2-position door checks. **REAR OPENING**—48" wide, 46.7" high.
6½-FT. PLATFORM & STAKE BODY	**LOAD SPACE**—platform: 84.3" long x 71.28" wide; stake 80" long, 67" wide, 29.54" high stakes. **LOADING HEIGHT** — 32.64" with 6.50-16 tires.	**PLATFORM**—bridge-type construction; heavy-gage steel framing riveted to cross girders; sturdy wood floor protected, interlocked by steel skid strips.	**STAKE RACKS**—removable; sturdy, straight-grained wood; one-piece side and end sections.	**RUB RAIL**—steel, around platform; steel caps on ends of body sills. **POCKETS**—flush with floor; welded to inside of frame rail, riveted to outside.

These specifications were in effect at the time this folder was approved for printing. The Ford Division of the Ford Motor Company, whose policy is one of continuous improvement, reserves the right, however, to discontinue models or change at any time, specifications, design or prices without notice and without incurring any obligation. Availability of equipment, accessories and trim is dependent on material supply conditions.

FORD Division of FORD MOTOR COMPANY • Dearborn, Michigan

FORD TRUCKING COSTS LESS BECAUSE FORD TRUCKS LAST LONGER!

Using latest registration data on 7,318,000 trucks, life insurance experts prove Ford Trucks last longer!

Much detail is contained in this listing. This one is dated April 1951.

were enough revisions to make people overlook the fact that the styling was beginning to look dated. When the 1951 models were introduced, Ford had already started on a replacement, a totally new design concept. By revising the models on hand, Ford hoped that it could still attract customers, at least until a new model could be released.

1952

Ford retooled its automobile lines for 1952, and there wasn't much money left for changes to the truck line. So buyers had to be satisfied with a few changes in this last model year for the 1948-style Ford truck. Not all the changes were small: Ford replaced the flathead six with a new overhead valve (ohv) version. This new, higher-compression engine (Cost Clipper) produced just as much power as the old flathead V-8, a fact that appealed to many buyers that year. It displaced only 215 cubic inches, versus 226 of its predecessor. The power of a V-8 with the economy of a six—that was a powerful marketing tool.

Economy savings were touted to be in the fourteen percent range (as compared to the old six). The V-8 version wasn't entirely left alone, as a new, higher-lift camshaft helped to boost power output. And with Power Pilot on tap, both engines were assured an economy reputation.

The 1952 Ford trucks were billed as The World's Greatest Trucks, a claim that was, at best, only an ad writer's dream. But these trucks *were* quite good, and they compared favorably to anything in their respective classes. They also looked better than most of their competitors.

The major change found on the 1951 Fords was their redesigned grille and grille cavity area. It's an easy way to distinguish them from the 1948-50 series, which used a series of horizontal bars in a slightly smaller grille cavity area.

Once again, Ford brought three series of light-duty trucks to the marketplace. The F-1 was billed as America's Number One, All Purpose, Utility Vehicle, noted for its economy of operation in general hauling use. The F-2 offered all the versatility of the F-1 plus added strength for hauling larger and heavier loads. The third series was the heavy-duty F-3, which was considered a leader in the low-price field for being able to operate under the most trying conditions. All these trucks were offered with quite a bit of standard equipment, a fact that Ford emphasized to its customers. And if the customer needed additional equipment, Ford made sure that its optional equipment was second to none.

The Five Star cabs returned in 1952 and Ford publicized them more that year for their comfort, convenience, visibility, safety and style. (Five stars; hence the Five Star name.) Also on hand was the Five Star Extra, a deluxe trim package that offered the buyer a slightly neater truck. This package consisted of foam-rubber seat padding (considered a luxury back in the early fifties on a truck), extra insulation throughout the cab for a quieter ride, chrome windshield molding and other pieces of brightwork, two-tone seat upholstery, deluxe door panel trim, dual sun visors, dual door locks, armrests, dome light and glovebox lock.

No matter which you chose, one thing

Ford truck catalogs of the period always presented their products in a dramatic fashion. After looking at this cover, nobody had a hard time recognizing a Ford. Ford Motor Company

was certain: Nobody could make a truck cab look more attractive than Ford. Some of the changes were just cosmetic in nature, most of them in the trim department. In front, the Ford name was taken out of the vent molding trim, and separate letters were once again affixed to the upper grille support panel, as they had been on the 1948-50 models. In the center of that vent, a chromed V-8 emblem was installed on those models so equipped. A change was also made to the hood's side trim molding, and the model designation (F-1, F-2) became part of this trim, instead of being attached separately on the cowl panel.

Ford claimed its 1952 trucks were "engineered to cost still less to run," and that they offered the buyer more power, more economy, more capacity, more comfort, more durability and more performance.

Sales dropped in that final year to only 138,000 units. The main reason for this decline may have been an extended steel strike, which lowered stocks. With no steel on hand, Ford and the others couldn't build trucks fast enough to meet demand, so some folks had to wait for their pickups for quite a while.

Here we see a 1952 International Harvester pickup loaded with supplies, posed at a 1952 construction site. Applegate & Applegate

At the end of the model year, the last of the F-1, F-2 and F-3 models rolled out the doors. In five model years, Ford had produced over 841,000 of these trucks—a respectable figure by anybody's standards. Ford's first postwar truck styling exercise was a tremendous success. That was quite an accomplishment for a company that just a short time before was floundering on the rocks. No one guessed at the time, when the first sketches were drawn, that these newly styled vehicles would help save the Ford Motor Company and launch it into transition—from a failing company into a company that was once again financially and commercially successful.

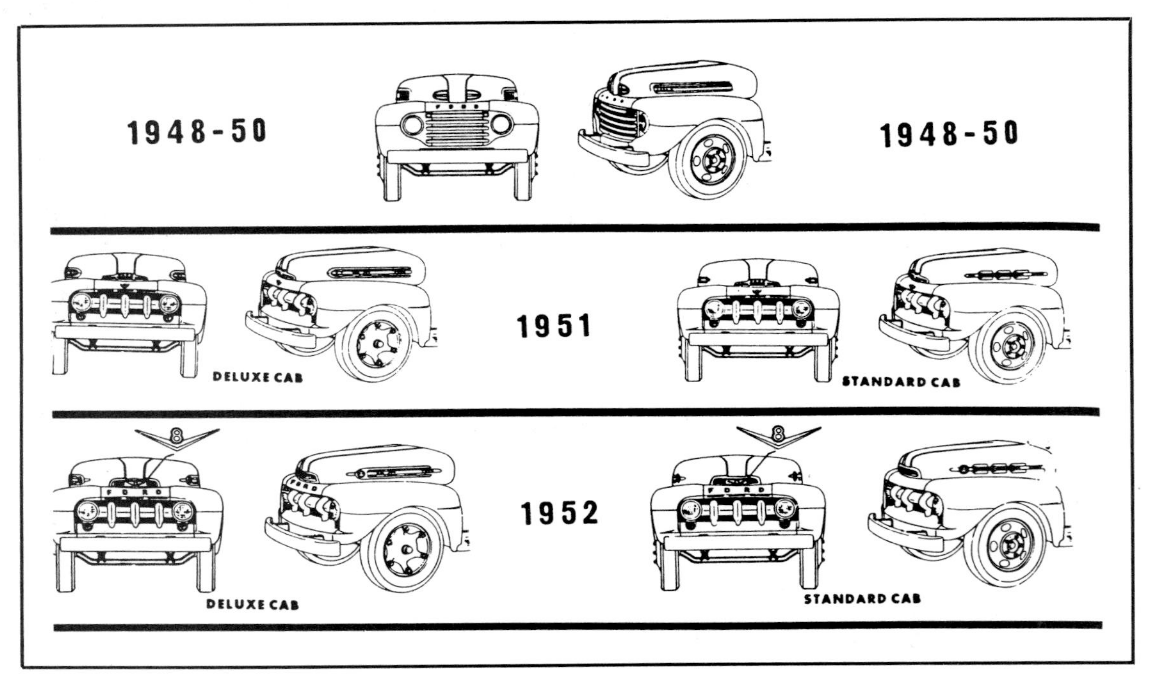

Instant recognition of the pre-1953 models taken from the back cover of Old Timer Auto Parts.

January 20, 1950
Page 1

1950 FORD BONUS BUILT TRUCK DATA

ENGINE DATA

	ROUGE 226 TRUCK SIX	ROUGE 239 TRUCK V-8	ROUGE 254 TRUCK SIX	ROUGE 337 TRUCK V-8
Max Gross Horsepower	95 @ 3300 RPM	100 @ 3800 RPM	110 @ 3400 RPM	145 @ 3600 RPM
Max Gross Torque	180 pound feet @ 1200 RPM	180 pound feet @ 1200 RPM	212 pound feet @ 1200 RPM	255 pound feet @ 1800 RPM
Bore and Stroke	3.3" x 4.4"	3.19" x 3.75"	3.5" x 4.4"	3.5" x 4.375"
Compression Ratio	6.8	6.8	6.8	6.4
Displacement	226 Cu. In.	239 Cu. In.	254 Cu. In.	337 Cu. In.
Taxable Horsepower	26.1	32.5	29.4	39.2

Starting Engine Numbers:

Conventional Trucks

Series F-1	97HC-92251	98RC-73088	-	-
Series F-2 and F-3	97HY-92251	98RY-73088	-	-
Series F-3 Par.Dely.	98HJ-92251	-	-	-
Series F-4,F-5 & F-6	97HT-92251	98RT-73088	-	-
Series F-6	-	-	9MTH-101	-
Series F-7 and F-8	-	-	-	98EQ-15174

Cab Over Engine Trucks

Series F-5 & F-6	97HW-92251	98RT-73088	-	-
Series F-6	-	-	9MWH-101	-

No colorful brochure this time, just a duplicated sheet for engine data in 1950.

MAKE	MODEL	LIST * PRICE	FACTORY ** RETAIL PRICE	MAXIMUM GROSS VEHICLE WEIGHT	SHIPPING WEIGHT
F-1 SERIES 114" LIGHT DUTY TRUCKS 1/2 TON 6 CYLINDER					
Pickup	9HC	1175.00	1255.50	4700	3025
Stake	9HC	1255.00	1338.00	4700	3095
Platform	9HC	1220.00	1301.50	4700	2975
Panel	9HC	1370.00	1457.50	4700	3195
Chassis Cab	9HC	1110.00	1187.50	4700	2645
Chassis Windshield	9HC	930.00	1001.00	4700	2175
Chassis Cowl	9HC	895.00	964.50	4700	2145
F-1 SERIES 114" LIGHT DUTY TRUCKS 1/2 TON 8-CYLINDER					
Pickup	9RC	1205.00	1286.50	4700	3065
Stake	9RC	1285.00	1369.00	4700	3135
Platform	9RC	1250.00	1333.00	4700	3015
Panel	9RC	1400.00	1489.00	4700	3235
Chassis Cab	9RC	1140.00	1218.50	4700	2685
Chassis Windshield	9RC	960.00	1032.00	4700	2215
Chassis Cowl	9RC	925.00	995.50	4700	2185
F-2 SERIES 122" LIGHT DUTY TRUCKS 3/4 TON 6-CYLINDER					
Express	9HD	1295.00	1382.50	5700	3520
Stake	9HD	1365.00	1455.00	5700	3640
Platform	9HD	1310.00	1398.00	5700	3450
Chassis Cab	9HD	1210.00	1292.50	5700	3040
Chassis Windshield	9HD	1030	1106.00	5700	2580
Chassis Cowl	9HD	995.00	1069.50	5700	2550
F-2 SERIES 122" LIGHT DUTY TRUCKS 3/4 TON 8-CYLINDER					
Express	9RD	1325.00	1413.50	5700	3560
Stake	9RD	1395.00	1486.00	5700	3680
Platform	9RD	1340.00	1429.00	5700	3490
Chassis Cab	9RD	1240.00	1323.50	5700	3080
Chassis Windshield	9RD	1060.00	1137.00	5700	2620
Chassis Cowl	9RD	1025.00	1100.50	5700	2590
F-3 SERIES 122" LIGHT DUTY TRUCKS 3/4 TON HEAVY DUTY 6-CYLINDER					
Express	9HY	1380.00	1472.00	6800	3770
Stake	9HY	1450.00	1544.50	6800	3870
Platform	9HY	1395.00	1488.00	6800	3680
Chassis Cab	9HY	1295.00	1382.00	6800	3270
Chassis Windshield	9HY	1115.00	1195.50	6800	2810
Chassis Cowl	9HY	1080.00	1159.00	6800	2780

MAKE	MODEL	LIST* PRICE	FACTORY ** RETAIL PRICE	MAXIMUM GROSS VEHICLE WEIGHT	SHIPPING WEIGHT
F-3 SERIES 122" LIGHT DUTY TRUCK 3/4 TON HEAVY DUTY 8-CYLINDER					
Express	9RY	1410.00	1503.00	6800	3810
Stake	9RY	1480.00	1575.50	6800	3910
Platform	9RY	1425.00	1519.00	6800	3720
Chassis Cab	9RY	1325.00	1413.00	6800	3310
Chassis Windshield	9RY	1145.00	1226.50	6800	2850
Chassis Cowl	9RY	1110.00	1190.00	6800	2820
F-3 SERIES 104" PARCEL DELIVERY TRUCK 6-CYLINDER					
Windshield front end	9HJ	1375.00	1463.50	7800	2940
F-3 SERIES 122" PARCEL DELIVERY TRUCK 6-CYLINDER					
Windshield front end	9H2J	1390.00	1479.00	7800	3010
F-4 SERIES 134" LIGHT DUTY TRUCKS 1 TON 6-CYLINDER					
Stake	9HTL	1530.00	1628.00	10000	4785
Platform	9HTL	1475.00	1571.00	10000	4445
Chassis Cab	9HTL	1340.00	1430.50	10000	3765
Chassis Windshield	9HTL	1160.00	1243.50	10000	3375
Chassis Cowl	9HTL	1125.00	1207.50	10000	3345
F-4 SERIES 134" LIGHT DUTY TRUCKS 1 TON 8-CYLINDER					
Stake	9RTL	1560.00	1659.00	10000	4825
Platform	9RTL	1505.00	1602.00	10000	4485
Chassis Cab	9RTL	1370.00	1461.50	10000	3805
Chassis Windshield	9RTL	1190.00	1274.50	10000	3415
Chassis Cowl	9RTL	1155.00	1238.50	10000	3385
F-5 SERIES 134" HEAVY DUTY TRUCKS 1 1/2 TON 6-CYLINDER					
Stake	9HT	1570.00	1671.00	14000	5105
Platform	9HT	1515.00	1613.50	14000	4765
Chassis Cab	9HT	1380.00	1473.50	14000	4085
Chassis Windshield	9HT	1200.00	1286.00	14000	3635
Chassis Cowl	9HT	1165.00	1250.00	14000	3605
F-5 SERIES 134" HEAVY DUTY TRUCKS 1 1/2 TON 8-CYLINDER					
Stake	9RT	1600.00	1702.00	14000	5145
Platform	9RT	1545	1644.50	14000	4805
Chassis Cab	9RT	1410.00	1504.50	14000	4125
Chassis Windshield	9RT	1230.00	1317.00	14000	3675
Chassis Cowl	9RT	1195.00	1281.00	14000	3645

Chapter 2

Looking back: the later years, 1953-56

1953

This was a golden year for the Ford Motor Company, as it celebrated its fiftieth year in the automotive business. It was a very special year for the company, its people and its products. The previous year had brought major changes to the car lines, so changes in this realm were kept to a minimum. However, the truck line saw its biggest change in over twenty years. The commercial vehicles that had come before bore hardly any resemblance to the commercial vehicles that were released in 1953.

Taken from Clues *(from your friend the Ford dealer) in September 1953. All the shots emphasize driver space.*

Right after the 1948 series was released, the Ford people began planning an all-new line to make its debut in the mid-fifties. They planned an extensive revamping that they hoped would place the company in a position of truck leadership. During the following five years they spent approximately fifty million dollars on research and development, tool and die changes, design work, marketing and sales promotion. When these new trucks were released to the public on March 13, 1953, it was readily apparent that Ford had spent all that money wisely. These new vehicles received critical acclaim for their styling, and early sales figures showed they were an unqualified success. They were "classics in their own right," with looks that were right for the times, that had an endearing quality and a timelessness—looks that are as fresh today as they were over thirty years ago.

A lot of that development money went into creating better cabs for these new trucks. Ford felt that no matter how good a truck was, if the driver wasn't comfortable driving it he or she wouldn't come back when it was time to buy a new one. And Ford wanted to ensure that once a buyer was in the Ford camp, he or she stayed there.

The new trucks were built around a comfortable cab package. A box with measurements was specified, and into that space the seat was placed in relation to the instrument panel. (Although not recognized as such, at that time, this was probably the first practical use of the science of ergonomics.) Ford also began to use mannequins in developing its interiors. These mannequins were used to design a seat that could accommodate three adults comfortably. They were also used to find out how high to place the seat so that a driver could sit above other drivers and better see traffic. To further ease the driver's burden, the seat was placed on adjustable tracks that allowed a fore and aft movement of over four inches. In addition, the backrest was adjustable to fit a small driver, as well as a larger one.

Also for 1953 models, Ford enlarged the glass area around the cab, making it safer and more well lit. These cabs probably had more

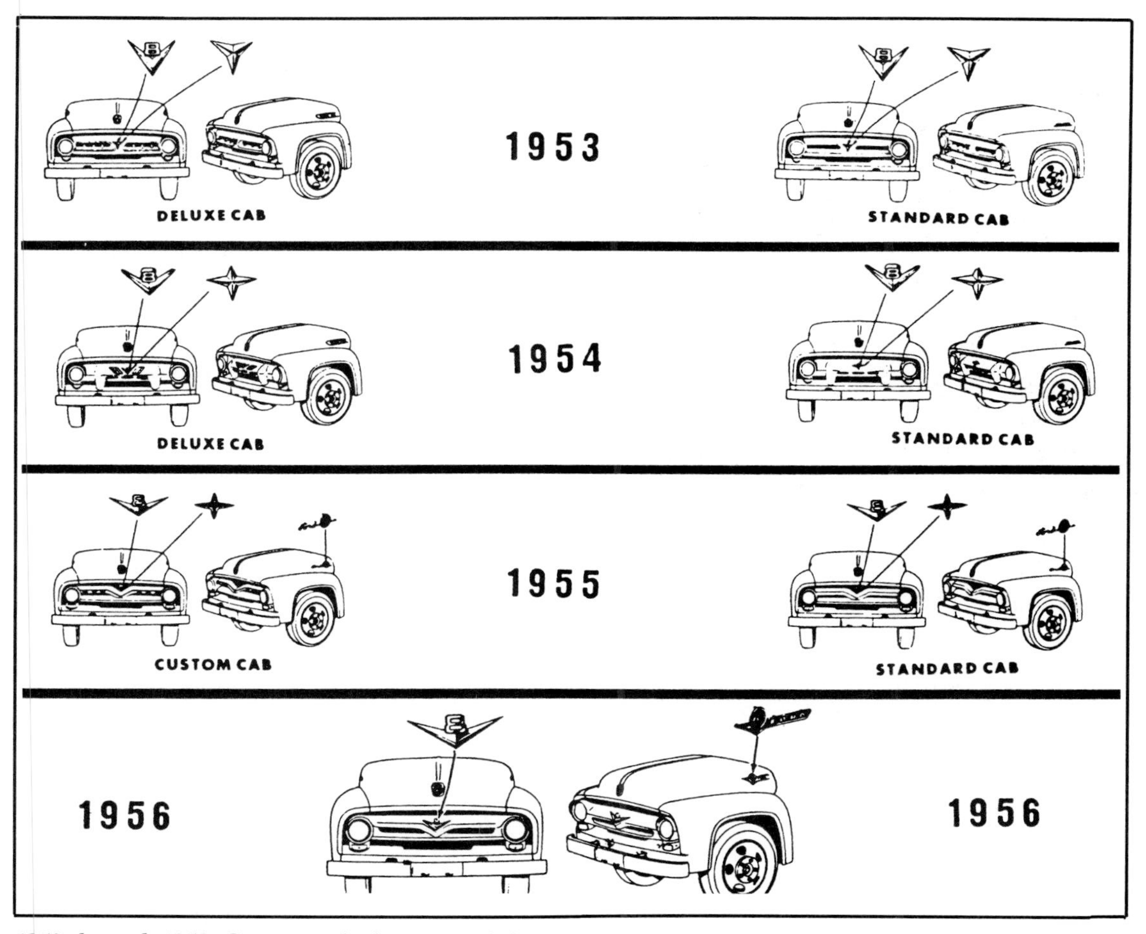

1953 through 1956. Compare the basic visual differences with the similar drawings for the 1948 through 1952 styles.

glass area than anything else in their class, which also increased visibility. The cab was taller and wider, making for more headroom and elbowroom. The doors were wider too, making ingress and egress much easier for the driver and passengers. Driver input was also used to set the steering wheel position and column angle, as well as the central grouping of the fully gauged instrument cluster, right in front of the driver. The end result of all this effort was Ford's claim to have the best "driverized" cabs on the market.

While the interior specifications were modified, the exterior shapes were being developed. It was decided early on to develop a new design from a clean sheet of paper, so all the older ideas were shelved. The new parameters called for building a bigger truck in a smaller overall package as compared to the earlier series. This meant the need for new fenders (front and rear), new hood, new grille cavity, new running boards, new pickup bed, new chassis and at least a thousand other changes. It was a very tall order, but the Ford people came through and developed a sweet little truck.

This new venture needed its own special identity. Ford stylists outdid themselves by creating one of the most handsome crests to ever appear on any vehicle, let alone one of such common heritage. The crest was similar in shape to the Ford car crest that had been introduced in 1950. The surround was chrome brightwork; at the top of the crest, in dark letters, the word Ford appeared. In the center, superimposed over a red field, was a chrome gear speared by a chrome lightning bolt. The combination was very striking, and

This prototype interior shot was photographed in mid-1952. (Note the Lincoln in the background.) This is a 1953 standard cab. Ford Motor Company

1953 hood nameplate.

This 1953 was found at the 1985 North/South Run in Fresno, California.

June 1953 is the publication date of this brochure cover. Once again the drivers are dwarfed by their trucks.

All New Comfort Ride—in Every Way!

ALL-NEW
DRIVERIZED
CABS
Deluxe shown

New One-piece Curved Windshield, 55% bigger for more visibility. Full-width rear window—4 ft. wide! Deep side windows.

All-New Roominess everywhere you look! With wider cab interiors, there's more hip room, shoulder room, leg room and foot room!

New Curved Instrument Panel has "cockpit" cluster with big instruments for split-second reading. Smart new interior trim.

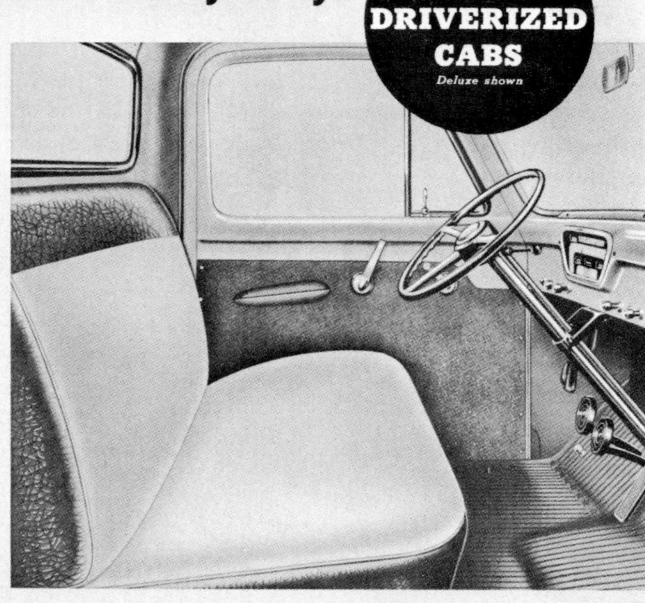

Roomiest, Most Comfortable Truck Cabs on the American Road . . . Designed to Reduce Driving Fatigue!

The all new Ford *Driverized* Cabs usher in a completely new era of truck riding comfort. They ride so easily, you handle the controls so easily, you won't believe you're riding in a truck. Every inch of these new Ford Cabs is designed to free the driver of truck fatigue . . . to make driving easier, safer and more efficient. There's more roominess, more comfort, more convenience, more visibility! Less effort required for driving means drivers stay fresh longer, like their jobs better, do more and better work.

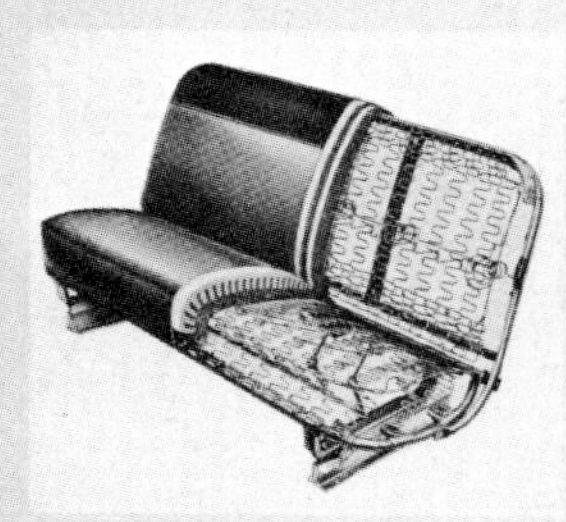

New Wider Seat provides roomy comfort for 3 men. New non-sag springs. *Exclusive* Ford Counter-Shock seat snubber absorbs road shocks for a softer, smoother ride. Both seat and seat back are independently adjustable.

New Wider Door Opening for easy entrance and exit. New goose-neck hinges swing door outside door opening, hold door firmly for better fit. More space between seat and door pillar lets driver swing in and out with ease.

DRIVERIZED DELUXE CAB . . . **FINEST TRUCK CAB EVER BUILT!**

For slight additional cost, you receive all these customized "extras"!

Foam rubber seat padding! Thermacoustic headlining, backed by glass wool insulation! Sound deadener on floor and rear panels! Two-tone seat upholstery and interior trim! Two sun visors! Two arm rests! Cigar lighter! Dome light with automatic door switches! Lock on dispatch box and both doors! Twin, electric horns! Distinctive chrome or bright metal hardware and exterior trim!

NEW FEATURES EVERYWHERE!

3-Way ventilation for fresh, clean air! New deeper arm-rest side windows! Improved Level-Action suspension! Fully weather-sealed construction! New insulation keeps out engine fumes! New overlapping windshield wipers! New push-button door handles! New Rotor-type door latches! New MagicAire heating, defrosting and ventilating system—most efficient in any truck (extra cost)! New stronger doors and pillar posts! Sound deadener on doors! Ideally located clutch and brake pedals!

Ford was emphatic about giving the driver a better time in Ford trucks. This is a full page from a 1953 brochure.

this proud badge remained the Ford truck symbol for many years. It was this attention to detail that helped make these mid-fifties Ford trucks so appealing. All Ford cars and trucks built that year also featured a "50th Anniversary, 1903-1953" horn button.

Another 1953 change occurred in the model designations: The F-1, Ford's half-ton, became the F-100; the F-2, the three-quarter-ton, became the F-250; the F-3, three-quarter-ton heavy-duty, became the F-350; and so on. All Ford trucks this year, in all ranges, received new designations.

When the new Ford truck lineup made its debut on March 13, 1953, the public noticed right away that it was quite different from anything that had come before. The product line was totally new and in stark contrast to the competition's offerings. From the public's standpoint, Ford had wisely spent that fifty million dollars, and customers spoke their approval by visiting their Ford dealers and placing orders.

The first thing one noticed was the size; these trucks were massive looking, even in the light-duty range. This illusion was helped by the larger cab, shorter wheelbase, shorter overall length, wider track, flatter hood and bulbous front fenders. The shorter wheelbase and shorter length also made for a shorter turning circle and an easier-driving truck. The competition decried these traits, saying that the trucks would be rougher riding. Ford took care of that possible problem by redesigning springs, shocks and axles. The result was a truck that rode better than most, carried more payload and was easier to drive, especially in the tight confines of city driving. The new Ford trucks developed a reputation for being the sweetest-handling trucks of their time. And they still ride and handle well in comparison to some of the trucks around today.

This 1953 Chevrolet promotional photograph features a pickup with the big rear window and lots of chrome trim. Applegate & Applegate

One thing the Ford truck people didn't change was the long list of standard equipment that was included in the base price. Many of these items were either not found on competitive makes or were found at extra charge. Base prices ranged from a low of $1,012 for a stripped F-100 cowl-and-chassis model to a high of $1,700 for an F-350 stake body. Between these two price extremes, there were about forty models offering something for just about everybody.

If you weren't satisfied with a base model, Ford once again offered a deluxe cab option that included various upgrades, including sound-deadening materials throughout the cab, more comfortable foam-rubber seat padding, bright two-tone seat upholstery, twin electric horns, dome light with automatic door switches, door and glovebox locks, twin visors, and a host of brightmetal trim on the interior as well as on the exterior. All of this resulted in one handsome cab, surely one of the best in the business.

Not changed were the powertrain systems, which were carried over from 1952. The Cost Clipper six offered 101 horses and 185 pounds-feet of torque from its 215 cubic inches of displacement. It was a real workhorse, offering power along with economy. And its efficient overhead valve arrangement had it putting out almost as much horsepower as the flathead V-8. (The venerable flathead V-8 made its last appearance in US Ford cars or trucks during this model year.) The light commercial version still displaced 239 cubic inches and put out about 106 horsepower. With figures like that, it was no wonder people preferred the six.

Backing up the engines were five transmission choices. Three were carried over from the previous year, while the two additions gave Ford the broadest range of transmission choices in its market segment. Three versions, a regular three-speed manual, a heavy-duty three-speed manual and a new three-speed manual with overdrive, had their

Drive your old truck through our door and . . .

watch its value go up!

COLLINGSWORTH MOTOR CO.

805 9th St. • Phone 228

Wellington, Texas

23—173

Clues, *December 1953*

The famous Ford truck crest made its original appearance on the 1953 models. It consisted of a gear bisected by a bolt of lightning—appropriate, to symbolize power!

shifting mechanisms located on the column, making for more footroom in the cab. The four-speed manual shifter was still located on the floor, in true truck fashion. The fifth version was an automatic transmission, the first time such an option was offered in a Ford truck. This transmission was a beefed-up version of Ford's three-speed Ford-O-Matic with the shifter and quadrant located on the column.

Other good news was the addition of synchronizers on all gears, in the manual boxes above first gear. This enabled smoother shifting without double clutching, which appealed to many drivers, especially those who had to deal with stop-and-go city driving.

With an automatic transmission available, no double clutching, a choice of V-8 or six, plus new styling and creature comforts, there was no doubt that America's #1 Economy Trucks of 1953 offered buyers a lot of truck for their money. And the buyers responded by purchasing 177,800 of these Ford light commercial vehicles. The darling of the bunch was the F-100, which sold over 116,400 units.

1954

It was more of the same for 1954, except for some minor changes in trim and grillework. The only change of any significance was in the powertrain department, where the venerable flattie V-8, around since 1932, was finally replaced by a modern overhead valve V-8 of the same 239 cubic inch displacement. By going to the ohv layout, Ford could offer an engine that provided better breathing and more power potential over a broader rpm spectrum. These engines were more efficient because they were designed with a larger bore and a shorter stroke. In that way the engine operated with less frictional power

Styling changes to Studebaker trucks were kept to a minimum from 1949 to 1956. This 1954 model, photographed at the Studebaker works, features a new headlight and grille frontpiece; otherwise it shares everything else with earlier and later models. Applegate & Applegate

loss (since the piston didn't have to travel as far), and with more power on tap at a lower rpm the engines were more economical.

These new engines were called Y-block V-8's because the engine block extended below the centerline of the crankshaft, creating a more rigid, stronger bottom end. In addition, the crankshaft was supported by five main bearings instead of the previous three. Thus, the engines were stronger and ran smoother.

Another result of using the ohv was that combustion chambers could be designed smaller, which increased compression ratios, which in turn increased power output—so the 239 Y-block got a boost of twenty-four horsepower over its L-head counterpart and was rated at 130. The Cost Clipper six got a boost in compression ratio and cubic inches too; to 115 horses and 223 cubic inches.

Ford again offered an artist's palette of bright exterior colors, including Raven Black, Sheridan Blue, Glacier Blue, Sea Haze Green, Vermilion (red), Meadow Green and Goldenrod Yellow. Most of these colors were carried over from the previous year.

Note slanted windshield posts and matching doors on this 1954 F-100. From 1953 through 1955, all Ford trucks featured these slanted posts, but in 1956 these posts and doors were modified to provide for a wraparound windshield.

One other change concerned prices which, overall, were about $100 more per model. Also, even more convenience items were added to the option list, including power brakes (vacuum assisted) and power steering.

Model year output for Ford's light commercial vehicle lineup was down somewhat at 157,000 units, of which 101,000 or so were F-100 pickups, again the most popular model. The fact that sales dropped was probably because there really wasn't anything to differentiate a 1954 from a 1953.

1955

For 1955, Ford decided to really go after the truck market. Management people knew that Chevrolet would be introducing a newly styled truck at mid-year, and if Ford wanted to keep its market share it had better keep on its toes. Most of us believe that a strong offense is the best defense, and Ford followed that rule to the letter. Its sales and marketing people got down to brass tacks by promoting Ford products as Money Makers featuring Triple Economy.

The first economy dealt with Ford's short-stroke engines that provided power with gas-saving economy. They played on the idea that a piston doesn't have to travel as far in a short-stroke design as in a long-stroke design to produce the same amount of power. Convenience of operation was given as the second economy; Ford's driverized cabs con-

1954 hood nameplate.

International Harvester always had a reputation for building stout trucks, a reputation that included its light-duty line. This 1955 model is equipped with four-wheel drive. Applegate & Applegate

This promotional photo was probably shot at the Ford Motor Company test track. The 1955 F-100 was one of the best designs during the 1953-56 era. Ford Motor Company

tained more of the creature comforts that allowed the driver to do a better job with fewer actions. And strength was given as the third economy; Ford trucks were designed to be stronger than their counterparts, allowing for larger and heavier payloads which resulted in fewer trips. (These items seem foreign to today's truck buyer but one has to remember that back then, most trucks were sold to commercial interests, rather than the broader truck market of today that includes, for example, a tremendous recreational vehicle segment.)

This year, 6-volt electrics were used. And from the inside out, the Ford V-8 engines got a power boost, mostly due to another compression ratio boost. Set at 7.5:1, the 239 ohv Y-block V-8 produced 132 horses at 4200 rpm. For six-cylinder buyers, the 223 cubic inch engine was called the Mileage Maker six. It produced 118 horsepower at 3800 rpm, and it featured a 7.5:1 compression ratio. With the higher compression ratios, Ford was able to coax more power out of its engines with the same economy. "Make money and save money with Ford's economy" were the watchwords of the day.

After two model years, Ford's driverized cabs were well known for their comfort, conveniences, roominess, visibility and safety. Ford decided to do still better by making these cabs more colorful and pleasant to look at. The seat was the same except it was covered in a better-looking vinyl. The rest of the standard cab retained the items that made Ford a leader in cabs: the large glass areas, the adjustable seat, and the centralized, easy-to-read instrument cluster.

Ford also offered a new Custom Cab option, which was a deluxe appearance

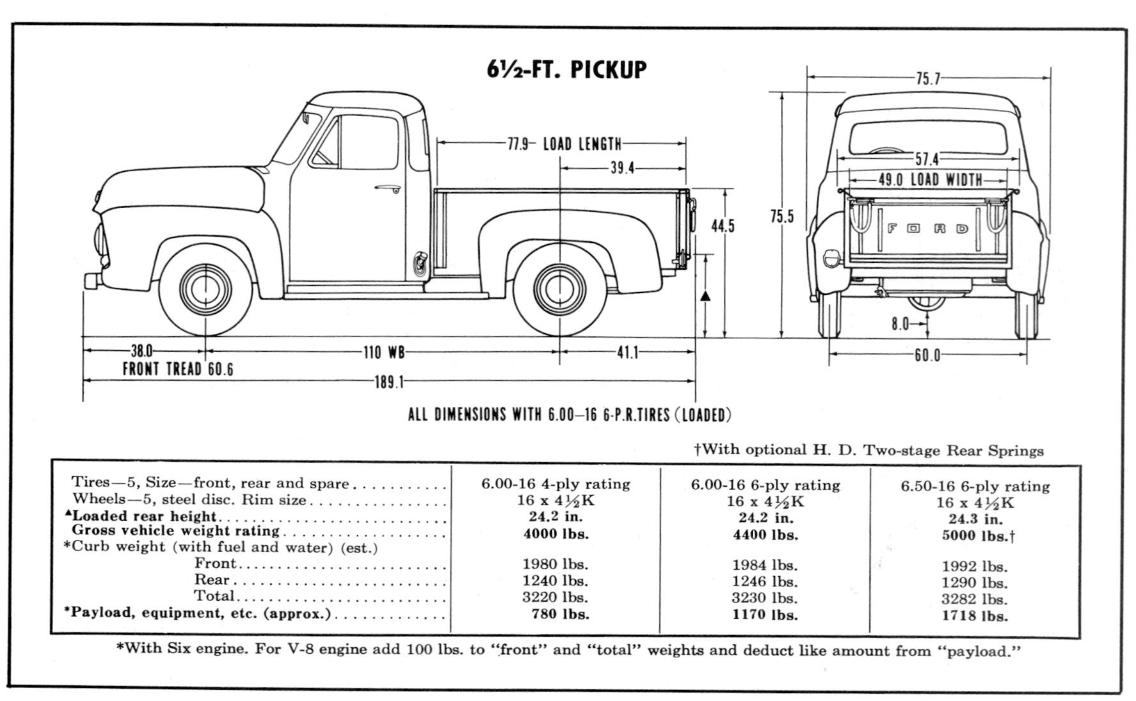

†With optional H. D. Two-stage Rear Springs

Tires—5, Size—front, rear and spare	6.00-16 4-ply rating	6.00-16 6-ply rating	6.50-16 6-ply rating
Wheels—5, steel disc. Rim size	16 x 4½K	16 x 4½K	16 x 4½K
▲Loaded rear height	**24.2 in.**	**24.2 in.**	**24.3 in.**
Gross vehicle weight rating	**4000 lbs.**	**4400 lbs.**	**5000 lbs.†**
*Curb weight (with fuel and water) (est.)			
Front	1980 lbs.	1984 lbs.	1992 lbs.
Rear	1240 lbs.	1246 lbs.	1290 lbs.
Total	3220 lbs.	3230 lbs.	3282 lbs.
***Payload, equipment, etc. (approx.)**	**780 lbs.**	**1170 lbs.**	**1718 lbs.**

*With Six engine. For V-8 engine add 100 lbs. to "front" and "total" weights and deduct like amount from "payload."

Body dimensions for 1955 model with 6½ foot truck bed.

Russell Barker is pretty proud of the fact that he still has the original service contract issued with his 1955 F-100 pickup. He also proudly displays the Prince Albert can found in the glovebox when he bought the truck. The truck is 100 percent stock.

upgrade package. In addition to the standard features, Ford offered color-keyed (red for some exterior combinations, green for others) two-tone upholstery. The seat side bolsters, door and kick panels, sun visors and headliner were done in a complementary shade of light gray. As before, the exterior color was carried over into the interior and was placed on all metal surfaces that didn't feature brightwork. The Custom Cab also included dual electric horns, sound-deadening material, deluxe door panels, armrests, dual visors, foam rubber pads in the seat and other interior goodies. On the outside, a brightmetal band was placed on the drip molding above the door. A Custom Cab plaque was affixed to the doors just below the windows, and brightwork was added to the grille area.

Another change noted on the 1955 truck lines was a new grille, which featured two horizontal bars, the top one vee'd in the middle. This vee'd area contained either a star (denoting a six-cylinder powerplant) or a V-8 symbol (denoting the use of a Power King engine). The grille bars were finished in a soft white.

With the following bright hues available, Ford was second to none in exterior colors: Black, Banner Blue, Aquatone Blue, Waterfall Blue, Snowshoe White, Sea Sprite Green,

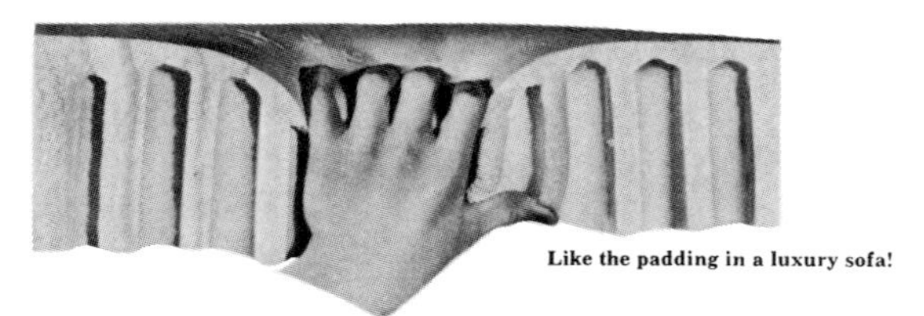

Foam rubber
5 soft inches thick

cushions you in Ford's new
***Custom Driverized* Cab**

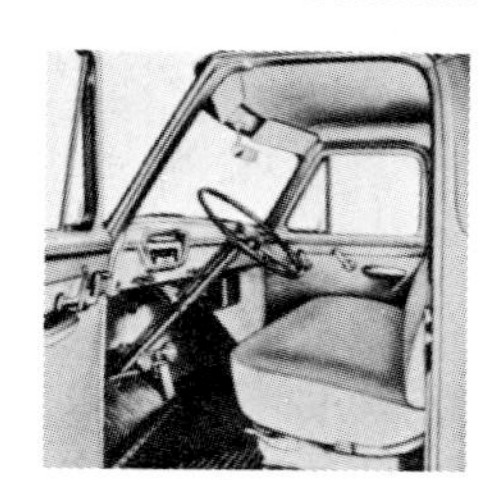

Curved one-piece windshield, total glass area of more than 2,100 square inches on all standard and *Custom* cabs. Doors almost a yard wide open to 70° angle. *Custom* Cab is shown

ONLY FORD offers so much working comfort — to help you get jobs done easier — to make Ford Trucks still more efficient MONEY MAKERS!

FORD'S new 1955 Driverized Cab, the most comfortable driver-saving truck cab ever built, features new free-breathing woven plastic upholstery, exclusive seat shock snubbers and non-sag seat springs as standard equipment. Among 17 "customized" extras in the new *Custom* Cab (low added cost) are new full foam-rubber cushioning, over five soft inches thick in seat, three inches in seat back . . . and new color-keyed, two-tone upholstery.

Ford Triple Economy Trucks
NEW MONEY MAKERS FOR '55

The Ford Motor Company mailed copies of its Clues *magazine to truck owners and buyers.* Clues, *January-February 1955*

The Custom Cab plate was affixed to the upper door area just below the window.

The Ford crest above the stylized star indicates this truck is of 1955 vintage. It's a standard version powered by a six-cylinder engine. Otherwise a V-8 emblem would replace the star and there would be more chrome trim for a deluxe version.

Torch Red, Meadow Green and Goldenrod Yellow. These choices were almost doubled by the two-tone offerings this year. The complementary color was Snowshoe White, which was used on the top panel and the upper rear cab panel. Snowshoe White was also used on the wheels on the F-100 vehicles that year. These trucks looked more colorful and probably more appealing than before.

The result of this more aggressive approach was that Ford sold quite a few light-duty trucks in 1955, and Ford's market share for all trucks increased by half a point, in spite of Chevrolet's new design. In the lightweight range, Ford sold over 191,500 vehicles, which was rather remarkable considering that it had to make do with the same overall package. There was no doubt about it, the marketplace found Ford's truck offerings more appealing this year. What kept people coming back to Ford was a growing reputation for quality, a fact that is no more apparent than in the trucking industry.

Nineteen hundred fifty-five was one of the best years the auto and trucking industries ever had. The manufacturers all hoped that 1956 would bring more of the same, and they worked just as hard to keep the momentum going. Ford had done extremely well against its arch rival, Chevrolet, especially in truck sales, in 1955. Ford was in the number-two position mostly because Chevrolet had more production facilities. Though Chevrolet had the upper edge in production numbers, Ford truck figures were cutting deeper into those sales figures each year. And it wasn't long before Ford surpassed Chevrolet for the top position, but it wasn't in 1955.

1956

This year, Chevrolet emphasized its power image in its Hot Ones promotional campaigns, while Ford pushed the safety aspects of its products, emphasizing its Lifeguard Designs, which included deep-dish steering wheels, padded dashes, strong door latches and seat belts.

This 1955 Chevrolet Cameo pickup is an example of the first "automobilized" pickup. Applegate & Applegate

For 1955, Ford in part took another tack to sell its light trucks. Farmers were always a good market and the thought of making your new truck into a money earner was more than many of them could resist.

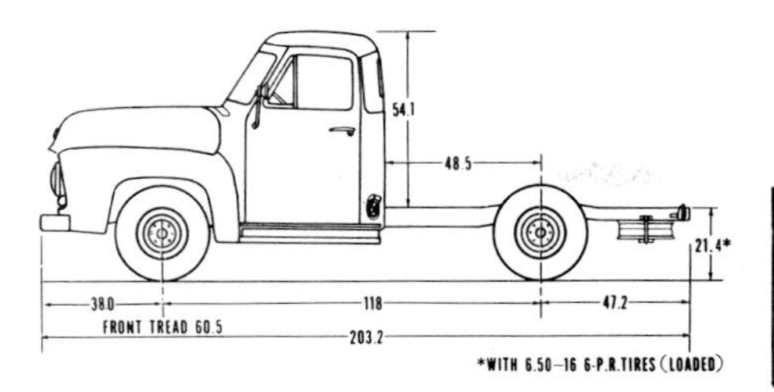

SERIES F-250 CHASSIS MODELS ESPECIALLY SUITED FOR CUSTOM-BUILT BODIES FROM 7 TO 8 FT.

Ford F-250 chassis-cab is available on 118-in. wheelbase for special-purpose, two-unit bodies to fit your loadspace requirements. Chassis-cowl and chassis-windshield also available for single-unit custom bodies. Body and payload capacity (with equipment and driver) goes up to 3,448 lbs. for the chassis-cab, up to 3,953 lbs. for the chassis-cowl.

CAPACITY CHART—SERIES F-250 CHASSIS WITH CAB

TIRES—4. SIZE—front and rear	6.50-16 6-p.r.	7.00-17 6-p.r.	7.50-17 8-p.r.
GROSS VEHICLE WEIGHT RATING (Severe Service Rating)	4900 lbs.	5800 lbs.†	6900 lbs.†
***CURB WEIGHT** (with fuel and water) (est.) front	2135 lbs.	2217 lbs.	2234 lbs.
rear	1080 lbs.	1201 lbs.	1218 lbs.
total	3215 lbs.	3418 lbs.	3452 lbs.
***PAYLOAD, BODY, EQUIPMENT, ETC.** (approx.)	1685 lbs.	2382 lbs.	3448 lbs.

**With Six engine. For V-8 engine, add 100 lbs. to "front" and "total" and deduct like amount from "payload."*
†With Optional H.D. Rear Springs.

F-250 SPECIFICATIONS

MAXIMUM GROSS VEHICLE WEIGHT 6,900 POUNDS

AXLE, FRONT
Capacity—lbs. 2600
Size (Height x Width x Web)—in. .... Modified I-Beam—2.29 x 1.67 x 0.32

AXLE, REAR
Capacity—lbs. 5000
Type .... Hypoid—Full Floating—4.86 to 1 ratio

BRAKES, SERVICE
Type .... Hydraulic, Two-Shoe, Single Anchor, Self-Energizing
Front and Rear Brake (Drum Diam. x Lining Width—Thickness)—in. .... 12 x 2—$\frac{3}{16}$
Total Area: Drum—Lining—sq. in. .... 302—196

BRAKE, HAND
Type .... Drum and Contracting Band at Rear of Transmission on Drive Line
Size (Drum Diam. x Lining Width—Thickness)—in. .... 8.0 x 2.0—$\frac{5}{32}$
Total Lining Area—sq. in. 49

BUMPER
Type .... Curved, Truck-Type Channel Bolted Direct to Front of Frame Side Rails

CLUTCH
Diameter, in.—Area, sq. in.: Standard .... 10— 85.5
Optional (extra cost) .... 11—123.7
Type .... Gyro-Grip, Semi-Centrifugal Single Plate
Clutch Disc .... Cushioned Hub with Vibration Damper
Release Bearing .... Sealed Ball, Pre-Lubricated
Attachment—Levers to Pressure Plate .... Needle Roller Bearings

COOLING SYSTEM
Capacity—qts. .... Six—18½; V-8—22
Radiator .... Flat Tube and Fin—Pressure Cap
Thermostat(s) .... In Engine Water Outlet(s)
Fan, 4-blade, Diameter—in. .... Six—18; V-8—18

DRIVE LINE
Type .... Hotchkiss, Straight-Line Drive
Propeller Shafts—Number .... Two, Tubular, Forged Steel Ends
Diameter, in. .... 2.0 (front)—2.5 (rear)
Universal Joints .... Three, Needle Roller Bearing
Center Bearing .... Rubber Encased Ball Type

ELECTRICAL SYSTEM
Battery .... 6-Volt, 17-Plate, 90-Amp. Hr. Capacity
Generator .... 35 Amp., 250 Watts
Ignition .... Full Vacuum Controlled System, Fully Automatic Distributor; Metal-Clad Coil; Open Wiring in Rubber Grommets with Moisture-Proof Boots over Spark Plugs
Headlights .... Sealed Beam, Foot-Switch Beam Control
Starter .... High Torque, Automatic Engagement, Solenoid Switch, Push-Button Control
Parking Lights; Left-hand Combination Stop and Tail Light; Instrument Lights; Ignition Switch with Key Lock; Circuit Breakers; Voltage Regulator.

ENGINES

	COST CLIPPER SIX	POWER KING V-8
Bore and Stroke, in.	3.62 x 3.60	3.50 x 3.10
Displacement—cu. in.	223	239
Max. Brake Horsepower—RPM	118 @ 3800	132 @ 4200
Max. Torque—Lbs.-Ft.—RPM	195 @ 1200-2400	215 @ 1800-2200
Compression Ratio	7.5 to 1	7.5 to 1

FRAME
Side Rails—Type .... Parallel, Channel Section—Tapered Front and Rear
Max. Section (Depth x Flange x Thick.)—in. .... 6.0 x 2.25 x 0.19
Cross Members .... 6—Flanged "U" Type and Channel Section
Section Modulus 3.34

FUEL SYSTEM
Carburetor .... Downdraft
Air Cleaner .... Heavy Duty Oil Bath, One Qt. Capacity
Fuel Pump and Filter .... Diaphragm Type, Driven from Camshaft
Fuel Tank—Chassis without Cab .... 17-Gal. Inside Left Frame Rail
Chassis with Cab .... 17-Gal. Outside Left Frame Rail Below Cab

LUBRICATION
Engine .... Full Pressure Feed to all Main, Crankpin and Camshaft Bearings
Crankcase Capacity (with opt. oil filter) .... 6 Qts. (dry); 5 Qts. (refill)
Chassis .... Fittings for Pressure Lubrication

SHOCK ABSORBERS
Front and Rear .... Direct, Double Acting, Telescopic

SPRINGS—Semi-Elliptic, Alloy Steel

	Front	*Rear*
Length x Width—in.	42 x 1.75	48 x 2.25
Number of Leaves and Defl. Rate—lbs. per in.	7—308	9—446
Capacity at Spring Pad (Normal Defl.)—Per Spring, lbs.	1050	1950

NOTE: With 7.00-17 6-p.r. and 7.50-17 8-p.r. tires, optional heavy duty rear springs are required—defl. rate 549 lbs. per in.; capacity at spring pad (normal deflection) 2400 lbs. per spring.

STEERING
Type .... Worm and Dual Row Needle Bearing Roller
Ratio .... 18.2 to 1
Wheel .... 18 in. Dia., 3-Spoke
Turning Circle Diameter, Right or Left—ft. 40.8
Tie Rod .... Ball Stud and Socket, Spring Loaded for Automatic Take-up of Wear, Equipped with Rubber Dust Shields

TRANSMISSION
Standard .... Heavy Duty 3-Speed Synchro-Silent, Steering Column Shift
Optional (extra cost) .... 4-Speed Synchro-Silent, Center Shift
Optional (extra cost) .... Fordomatic, Selector Lever on Steering Column

Gear Positions	*First*	*Second*	*Third*	*Fourth*	*Reverse*
Ratio (to 1): Std. H.D. 3-Speed	3.71	1.87	1.00	—	4.59
Opt. 4-Speed	6.40	3.09	1.69	1.00	7.82
*Opt. Fordomatic	2.44	1.48	1.00	—	2.00

*Converter stall torque ratio .... 2.1 to 1

WHEELS AND TIRES
Wheels—Standard .... Five—16-Inch Steel Disc with 0.56 in. Offset; 8 hole, 6.5 in. Dia. Bolt Circle
Rims—Size and Type .... 16 x 6L Drop Center
Standard Tires—Front and Rear .... Four—6.50-16 6-p.r.

STANDARD EQUIPMENT in addition to items specified above:

Center Cowl Ventilator
Curved Instrument Panel*
Speedometer
Water Temperature Gage
Oil Pressure Gage
Fuel Gage
Charge Indicator
Ash Receptacle
Dispatch Box
Choke Button
Light Switch
Single Electric Horn
One-piece Curved Windshield*
Dual Windshield Wipers*
Air Wing Ventilating Windows in Doors*
Sun Visor, Left Side*
Mirror, Rear View—Inside on Express; Left, Outside, Long Arm on Stake, Platform and Chassis-Cab
Door Lock, Right Side*
Running Boards—Long on Express; Short on Stake, Platform and Chassis-Cab
Rear Fenders (Express only)
Spare Tire Carrier under Frame (under Floor on Platform and Stake)
Mechanical Jack (1½ ton capacity) and Tools

NOTE: Running boards are not standard on chassis with cowl.
*Except Chassis-Cowl.

STANDARD COLORS
Choice of Raven Black, Banner Blue, Meadow Green, Vermilion, Goldenrod Yellow, Aquatone Blue, or Sea Sprite Green (on hood, fenders, cowl, cab, interior metal, bodies of Stake and Express). Snowshoe White is available on Custom Cab roof and upper rear panel in a two-tone color combination with standard colors. Painted black are frame, fuel tank and cap, running boards, outside mirror, door divider bar, vent window frame, tail lamp, springs, axles, wheels and bumper. Cowl models are painted prime unless standard color is specified.

AVAILABLE EQUIPMENT AND ACCESSORIES at extra cost:

Battery—120 Amp. Hr.
Bumper, Rear, for Express
Cab, Custom
Carrier—Spare Wheel, Side Mounted (Express only)
Clutch, 11-inch (for std. transmission)
Directional Turn Signals
Engine Compartment Lamp
Fire Extinguisher (1½ qt.)
Governors
Hand Brake Signal (for std. transmission)
Heater and Defroster—MagicAire System or Recirculating
Hub Caps
Locking Gas Tank Cap
Mirror, Outside Rear View—Right or Left, 6" adjustment
Mirror, Arm Braces
Oil Filter
Radiator, Heavy Duty
Radiator Grille Guard—Heavy Duty
Radio
Reflector Flares (3 in Kit) with Flags
Road Lamps
Seat Cover
Spotlight with Bracket
Springs, H.D. Rear
Stop Lamp
Tail Light—Right Hand
Tinted Glass
Tow Hooks
Transmissions—4-Speed (includes 11-inch clutch); Fordomatic
Visor
Windshield Washer
Windshield Wipers—Positive Action, Dual Electric
Wheels and Tires—
(4) 7.00-16 6-p.r. tires on std. wheels
(4) 7.00-17 6-p.r. tires* & (5) 17 x 5.50 wheels
(4) 7.50-17 8-p.r. tires* & (5) 17 x 5.50 wheels
Spare Tire
*Heavy Duty Rear Springs Required

These specifications were in effect at the time this folder was approved for printing. The Ford Division of the Ford Motor Co., whose policy is one of continuous improvement, reserves the right, however, to discontinue models or change at any time, specifications, design or prices without notice and without incurring any obligation. Availability of equipment, accessories and trim is dependent on material supply conditions.

FORD Division of FORD MOTOR COMPANY • DEARBORN, MICHIGAN

There's one right FORD TRUCK money maker for your job!

These 1955 specifications come straight from the back page of the brochure.

Sturdy chassis is engineered for greater dependability

1. Modern, short-stroke 118-h.p. *Cost Clipper* **Six** (shown), or 132-h.p. *Power King* **V-8.**

2. Ford **Power Pilot** fully automatic carburetor-distributor for most power from the least gas.

3. Air Cleaner, 1-qt. oil bath type, to prolong engine life.

4. Engine mounting rubber cushioned for long life, smooth operation; easier engine servicing.

5. Large cooling capacity flat tube and fin **radiator** with long-life U-type support.

6. Channel bumper attached to extended frame for greater protection and rigidity.

7. Long, easy-action **front springs**—double-wrapped rear eyes for safety, shackled at front for stable steering.

8. Set-back, wide-tread **front axle** for more stability, shorter turning. Saves maneuvering time and effort.

9. Tie rod ends are spring loaded, ball-socket type, with dust shields, for automatic wear take-up, longer life.

10. Double-acting **shock absorbers,** front and rear, for comfortable, level-ride control.

11. Battery is safely located away from engine heat.

12. Roll Action **steering** for quicker response, easier handling.

13. 10-in. Gyro-Grip **clutch** multiplies grip with increased speed; low pedal pressure, high plate pressure for easier operation, longer life. 11-in. size available for heavier duty requirements.

14. Straight-line drive, with large diameter tubular **propeller shafts** and improved rubber encased center bearing for smoother power flow, longer U-joint life.

15. Deep-channel **frame;** parallel side rails for greater stability, higher rigidity, easier engine servicing.

16. Wide-span **rear springs** provide soft, easy ride, empty or loaded.

17. Sturdy hypoid **rear axle** with big pinion for quietness and high strength. Full-floating construction; split-type housing tubes carrying the load, relieves axle shafts of bending stresses for long life.

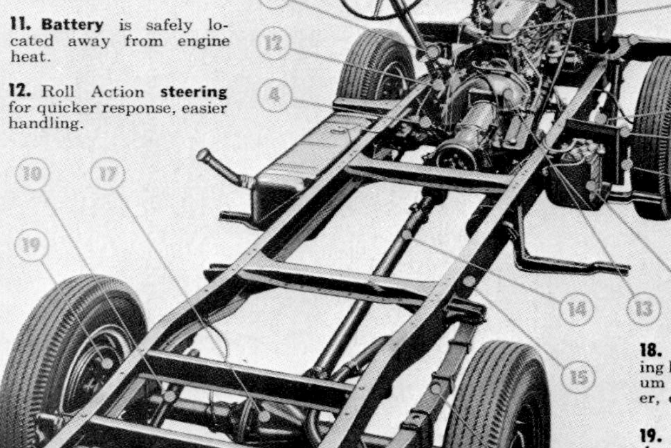

Chassis models available: Chassis with cab, with windshield, with cowl.

18. Powerful self-energizing hydraulic **brakes;** vacuum booster extra, for faster, easier stopping.

19. Removable **brake drums** for easier, lower-cost servicing.

20. Tire carrier mounted at rear; side mounted carrier for Express also available (extra cost).

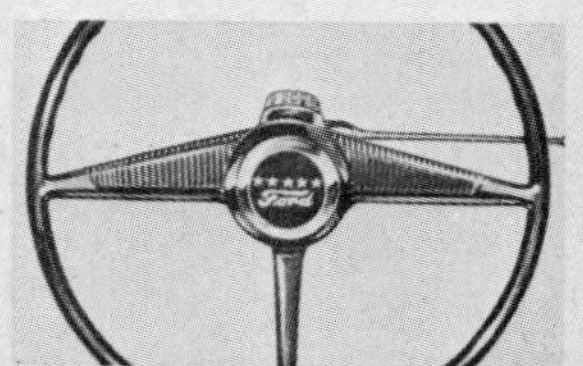

MORE VERSATILE FORDOMATIC DRIVE has new low gear "step down" for faster acceleration, more power at the start. Now smoother, quieter, sturdier—fully automatic *Fordomatic* provides exact adjustment to changing driving conditions. Negotiates over 30° grades with ease, even from a standing start. *Fordomatic* soon repays its low extra cost in time and effort saved.

STEERING COLUMN GEARSHIFT, for greater driving ease is included with the standard Heavy Duty 3-speed transmission Synchro-Silent. Its Synchro-Silent design makes for smooth, quiet, easy shifting with minimum driver effort, longer life. Provides greater safety in "down shifting." Also available, at extra cost, is a 4-speed Synchro-Silent Transmission, with center shift.

POWER BRAKING makes stopping up to 25% easier. Optional at extra cost, Power Braking boosts regular hydraulic actuation for smooth, fast stops with least effort and minimum pressure on the brake pedal. In fact, Power Braking requires less foot pressure to bring truck to a full stop, than would be needed to break an ordinary light bulb! A Ford *first* in the light-duty field!

Interesting chassis shot from the same 1955 sales brochure. Note the lightbulb under the braking foot, bottom right.

On the truck side of the ledger, this was the last year for the 1953 body style and Ford tried its best to dress up the offerings so it could claim some "newness." The 1956s were strictly transitional models, just marking time till the new models came on line. The biggest change occurred in the windshield area, where a new, wraparound version was featured. This change necessitated changes to the greenhouse, doors, dash area and roof panels. It was a rush job at best, but the result didn't look all that bad. As a matter of fact, most people prefer the looks of the 1956 models.

Once again, changes were made to the grille: For the first time since 1948, the factory offered a chrome grille on a Ford truck. Also, a new hood trim was featured. Another difference, which necessitated changing some dies, was in the back window area, where Ford offered a standard version and the Big Window option. The Big Window versions are highly sought after today by both hot rodders and restorers because of their lower production numbers and, some feel, better looks. Most Big Window models were found in the deluxe, Custom Cab range.

Powertrain offerings included the 223 Cost Cutter six, now producing 133 horsepower, made possible by another compression ratio boost. The V-8 version boasted 272 cubic inches and 167 horses, providing plenty of power on tap for hauling ease. The transmission choices now numbered six. New this year under the hood was the conversion to a 12-volt electrical system.

Once again Ford offered two levels of interior trim: standard and deluxe Custom Cab. Lifeguard Design features were available in both series. So one found a newly designed, deep-dish steering wheel; safety door latches to hold the doors shut in the event of an accident; and optional safety belts. There were few takers for the belts, much to Ford's chagrin. Besides the safety features, the 1956 cabs featured a redesigned instrument panel with a new cluster.

One-hundred-percent stock 1955.

1956 hood nameplate.

Note the radio antenna mounting on the cowl of this 1956 F-100.

For 1956, Ford revamped the upper cab and upper door area to allow its trucks to have wraparound windshields, an item that was in vogue in the mid- to late fifties.

This 1956 F-100 has hood hinge, hood chrome nameplate and chrome trim around the windshield and window.

1956 F-100 brake pedal, master cylinder and transmission mounting details.

Rear cab details on 1956 F-100 Big Window version. Note the side window chrome, which helps to brighten the looks of this cab.

The Custom Cab version included the same items and appointments as in the previous model years, plus one additional item, a fully chromed grille bar—a first for any Ford truck in almost ten years. It proved to be so popular that many standard-cab truck owners switched their cream grilles for the more

Detail shot of 1956 Custom Cab option with regular rear window.

1956 taillight and license plate details.

Features of the 1956 F-100 include taillights, bumper, tailgate, retaining chains and license plate mounting.

appealing chrome version. Who knows, if Ford had offered a chrome grille straight across the board the company might have been able to sell more trucks!

The Ford-O-Matic nameplate appears under the Ford crest on this hood front, indicating this 1956 F-100 is equipped with an automatic transmission.

Ford again offered an array of exterior colors that rivaled the rainbow. Color awareness was just starting to grow in the mid-fifties and Ford had some of the best selections. In 1956, the choices were Black, Nocturne Blue, Diamond Blue, Colonial White, Meadow Mist Green, Vermilion, Meadow Green, Golden Glow Yellow and Platinum Gray. In addition, the two-tone option was still available, with the roof and upper rear panel done in Colonial White. Colonial White was also the color found on F-100 wheels and on the standard cab's grille bar.

Ford had a model available for just about anybody's needs. The year 1956 turned out to be a recession year for the auto industry, with sales depressed in many market segments, but you wouldn't have known that by looking at Ford's light commercial vehicle sales performance, which reached a record-setting mark of just under 250,000. Some of the credit for that high number could be

This 1956 Ford promotional photograph shows a deluxe Custom Cab version. Note chrome trim around windows and the chrome grille which made its first appearance as an option in 1956.

attributed to the extended 1956 production run, which ran from September 1955 up to the introduction of the new 1957 models in February of 1957.

It might have been the last year for this particular body style, but Ford wasn't leaving this market as a loser, not by a long shot. In four years Ford had produced over 775,000 of these classic 1953-56 pickups and commercial vehicles. Many now feel that this era was the golden age of Ford truck production.

ALL LIGHT DUTY SPECIFICATIONS

ENGINE

133-H.P. Cost Cutter Six: Modern Short Stroke, overhead-valve, deep-block design. 3.62 in. bore x 3.60 in. stroke; 223 cu. in. displacement; max. gross horsepower: 133 @ 4000 rpm.; max. gross torque: 202 lbs.-ft. @ 1600-2600 rpm.; compression ratio: 8.0 to 1.

167-H.P. Power King Y-8: Modern Short Stroke, overhead-valve, deep-block design. 3.62 in. bore x 3.30 in. stroke; 272 cu. in. displacement; max. gross horsepower: 167 @ 4400 rpm.; max. gross torque: 260 lbs.-ft. @ 2400 rpm.; compression ratio: 8.0 to 1.

COOLING

Series-Flow System providing uniform coolant flow for increased velocity and closer temperature control. Positive-action thermostat in engine water outlet. Fan: 4-blade, 18" diameter. Flat tube and fin radiator with spherical top tank and pressure cap. Capacity of system: 18½ quarts (Six), 22 quarts (Y-8).

ELECTRICAL SYSTEM

12-volt system with high-capacity 66-plate, 55-amp. hr. battery and air-cooled 30-amp. generator. Circuit breakers, voltage regulator. Weatherproof ignition with fully automatic all-vacuum-controlled Power Pilot distributor, metal-clad coil and moistureproof boots over spark plugs. High torque starter, automatic engagement, solenoid switch, ignition key starter control. Sealed beam head lights with foot-switch beam control. Left-hand combination stop and tail light.

FUEL SYSTEM

Efficient downdraft carburetion. Automatic riser heat control. Heavy-duty one-quart capacity oil bath air cleaner std. on Y-8, oil-wetted type std. on Six. Diaphragm type fuel pump. Fuel tank 18-gallon capacity, inside cab behind seat back.

LUBRICATION

Positive full-pressure to all main, crankpin and camshaft bearings. Capacity: 6 quarts dry—5 quarts refill. Large-capacity gear-type pump. Directed-flow crankcase ventilation. Chassis fittings for pressure lubrication.

STANDARD EQUIPMENT: In addition to items specified below:

Center Cowl Ventilator
Curved Instrument Panel
Speedometer
Water Temperature Gage
Fuel Gage
Oil Pressure Warning Light
Generator charge Indicator Warning Light
Ash Receptacle
Dispatch Box
Choke Button
Light Switch
Single Electric Horn
Dual Windshield Wipers
Air Wing Ventilating Windows in Doors
Door Lock—Right Door
Sun Visor—Left Side
Mirror, Rear View—Inside Cab
Fenders, Rear
Running Boards—Long
Diagonal Type Spare Tire Carrier Under Frame
Mechanical Jack and Tools
Full-Wrap Windshield

STANDARD COLORS

Choice of Raven Black, Vermilion, Diamond Blue, Nocturne Blue, Meadowmist Green, Platinum Gray, Goldenglow Yellow or Meadow Green (on hood, fenders, cowl, bodies, running boards, fuel filler cap, and interior metal). Painted Black: Frame, tail lamp, springs, axle, door divider bar, vent window, frames, fuel tank, bumpers, and wheels (except Colonial White wheels on F-100). Colonial White is also available on Custom Cab roof and rear upper panel as a two-tone color combination with Standard body colors.

AVAILABLE EQUIPMENT AND ACCESSORIES: (at extra cost)

Battery—70 amp. hr.
Brakes—Vacuum Booster
Bumper, Rear
Cab, Custom
Directional Turn Signal and Class A Lights
Fire Extinguisher (1½ qt.)
Governors
Heater and Defroster—MagicAire System or Recirculating
Hood Ornament
Lifeguard Seat Belts
Locking Gas Tank Cap
Mirror, Outside Rear View, Right or Left, 6" adjustment
Mirror Arm Braces
Oil Filter
Radiator, Heavy-duty
Radiator Grille Guard—Heavy-duty
Radio—5 tubes plus rectifier, single knob control
Rear Window, Full-wrap
Reflector Flares (3 in Kit) with flags
Seat Cover
Splash Shields and Brackets
Spotlight with Bracket
Tail Light—Right Hand
Tinted Glass
Tire Lock, Side mounted carriers
Visor—outside
Windshield Washer
Windshield Wipers—positive-action, dual electric
Winter Windshield Wiper Blades

Note: For optional clutches, transmissions, wheels and tires, see Series Specifications

F-100 SPECIFICATIONS

AXLE, FRONT

Wide-track, heat-treated alloy steel forging with set-back design for shorter turning, better maneuverability. Capacity: 2600 lbs.

AXLE, REAR

Hypoid, semi-floating design with rigid integral-type housing; large diameter forged axle shafts with integral flanges. Capacity: 3300 lbs.

Ratios:		
3 or 4-spd. trans.	Six:	3.92 to 1
	Y-8:	3.73 to 1
Overdrive trans.	Six:	4.09 to 1
	Y-8:	3.92 to 1
Fordomatic trans.	Six:	3.92 to 1
	Y-8:	3.73 to 1

BRAKES

Hydraulic, two-shoe, single anchor, powerful self-energizing type, double-sealed front and rear brakes. Composite steel and cast iron drums, 11" diameter. Molded linings: width 2" front, 1¾" rear x 3/16" thick (all shoes except ¼" thick, secondary with Y-8 models), with large 179 sq. in. area for long lining life. Hand brake is grip handle on dash for actuation of rear brakes.

CLUTCH

Gyro-Grip, easy-action, semi-centrifugal design increases clutch plate pressure with engine speed. 10" diameter, 85.5 sq. in. frictional area with Six. 10.5" diameter, 96.2 sq. in. frictional area with Y-8. Opt. 11" dia. clutch available.

DRIVE LINE

Hotchkiss, straight-line drive. Tubular propeller shaft with forged steel ends and two highly-efficient, long-wearing needle roller bearing universal joints for 110" wb. With 118" wb. 8-ft. express. Hotchkiss straight-line drive, two tubular propeller shafts, with rubber-encased center bearing and three needle bearing universal joints.

FRAME

Truck-type with kick-up over rear axle for low loading height. 34" parallel channel side rails: depth 5.92", flange 2.25", thickness 0.15". Section Modulus 2.65. 4-Flanged "U" type cross members for 6½ ft. pickup and 110" wb. With 8-ft Express and 118" wb.: depth 6", flange 2.25", thickness 0.19". Section Modulus 3.34. 6-flanged "U" type cross members.

SHOCK ABSORBERS

Direct, double-acting telescopic design, front and rear, with rubber grommets at mountings.

SPRINGS

Wide-Span, semi-elliptic. Ford alloy steel. Front: 42" by 1¾", 8 leaves, deflection rate: 238 lbs. per inch. Capacity at pad (normal defl.): 950 lbs. each. Rear: 52" by 2", 6 leaves, with low deflection rate of 166 lbs. per inch for soft ride. Capacity at pad (normal defl.): 1025 lbs. each. Note: With 6.50-16 6-p.r. tires optional H.D. 9-leaf, 2-stage rear springs are required. Deflection rate: 172 and 258 lbs. per inch, capacity at pad (normal defl.): 1350 lbs. each.

STEERING

Worm and dual row needle bearing roller type with 18.2 to 1 ratio. 3-Spoke, 18" diameter steering wheel. Short-turning circle diameter (left or right) 37.1 ft. Tie rod ball stud and socket type with spring-loaded ends for automatic take-up of wear, equipped with rubber dust shields.

TRANSMISSIONS

Standard: Easy-Shifting 3-speed, all helical Synchro-Silent with steering column shift.

Optional (extra cost): 3-Speed M.D. Synchro-Silent or 3-Speed Synchro-Silent with Overdrive and steering column shift. Fordomatic with selector lever on steering column. 4-Speed Synchro-Silent with center shift.

WHEELS AND TIRES

Five 15-inch steel disc with 5K drop center rims. Five tubeless 6.70-15 4-p.r. tires standard.

Optional (extra cost): (5) 6.70-15 6-p.r. or (5) 7.10-15 6-p.r. with standard wheels; (5) 6.50-16 6-p.r. with 16 x 4½K wheels (two-stage rear springs required).

Independent insurance experts certify for the ninth straight year that Ford Trucks last longer! Actuarial studies of current license registrations . . . covering over 10,068,000 trucks of the five leading makes . . . show that *FORD TRUCKS LAST UP TO 9.9% LONGER THAN ANY OTHER LEADING MAKE!*

1956 specifications and the elephant shows up. Sales theme is still today much the same, "Ford Tough."

F-250 SPECIFICATIONS

AXLE, FRONT

Wide track, heat treated alloy steel forging with set-back design for shorter turning, better maneuverability. Capacity: 2600 lbs.

AXLE, REAR

Hypoid, full-floating design with rigid integral type housing; sturdy manganese steel axle shafts. Capacity: 5000 lbs.

Ratios:—Six Std. .... 4.88 to 1
V-8 Std. .... 4.56 to 1

BRAKES

Hydraulic, two-shoe, single anchor, powerful self-energizing type, single-sealed front and double-sealed rear brakes. Composite steel and cast iron drums: 12⅛" diameter. Molded linings: width 2" front and rear x 0.25" thick, with large 198 sq. in. area for long lining life. Hand brake: 8" x 2" spring-loaded drum type mounted on drive line back of transmission. Grip handle on dash.

CLUTCH

Gyro-Grip, easy-action, semi-centrifugal design increases clutch plate pressure with engine speed. 10" diameter, 85.5 sq. in. frictional area with Six. 10.5" diameter, 96.2 sq. in. frictional area with Y-8. Opt. 11" diameter clutch available.

DRIVE LINE

Hotchkiss, straight-line drive. Two tubular propeller shafts with forged steel ends and three highly efficient, long-wearing needle roller bearing universal joints with rubber-encased ball type center bearing.

FRAME

Truck-type with kick-up over rear axle for low loading height. 34" parallel channel side rails: depth 6", flange 2.25", thickness 0.19". Section Modulus 3.34. 6-Flanged "U" type channel section cross members.

SHOCK ABSORBERS

Direct, double-acting telescopic design, front and rear, with rubber grommets at mountings.

SPRINGS

Wide-Span, semi-elliptic. Ford alloy steel. Front: 42" by 1¾", 7 leaves, deflection rate: 308 lbs. per inch. Capacity at pad (normal defl.): 1050 lbs. each. Rear: 48" by 2¼", 9 leaves, deflection rate: 446 lbs. per inch. Capacity at pad (normal defl.): 1950 lbs. each. **Note:** With 8-19.5 8-p.r. tires, optional heavy duty rear springs are required. Defl. rate: 549 lbs. per in.; capacity at spring pad (normal defl.): 2400 lbs. per spring.

STEERING

Worm and dual row needle bearing roller type with 18.2 to 1 ratio. 3-Spoke, 18" diameter steering wheel. Short turning circle diameter (left or right): 40.7 ft. Tie rod ball stud and socket type with spring-loaded ends for automatic take-up of wear, equipped with rubber dust shields.

TRANSMISSIONS

Standard: Easy-Shifting Medium-Duty 3-Speed, Synchro-Silent with steering column shift.

Optional (extra cost): Fordomatic Drive with selector lever on steering column or 4-Speed Synchro-Silent with center shift.

WHEELS AND TIRES

Five 16-inch steel disc, with 6L drop center rims. Four tubeless 6.50-16 6-p.r. tires standard.

Optional (extra cost): (4) 7.00-16 6-p.r. with standard wheels, (4) 8-17.5 6-p.r. tires with (5) 17.5 x 5.25 wheels, or (4) 8-19.5 8-p.r. tires* with (5) 19.5 x 5.25 wheels.

**H.D. rear springs required.*

F-350 SPECIFICATIONS

AXLE, FRONT

Wide-track, heat-treated alloy steel forging with set-back design for shorter turning, better maneuverability. Capacity: 3200 lbs.

AXLE, REAR

Hypoid, full-floating design with rigid banjo-type housing; large diameter forged axle shafts with integral flanges. Capacity: 7200 lbs.

Ratios:—Six Std. .... 5.14 to 1
Opt. .... 5.83 to 1
V-8 Std. .... 4.86 to 1
Opt. .... 5.14 to 1

BRAKES

Hydraulic, two-shoe, single anchor, powerful self-energizing type, double-sealed front and rear brakes. Composite steel and cast iron drums, 12⅛" diam. front and 13" diam. rear. Molded linings: width 2" front, 2½" rear x ¼" thick, with large 231 sq. in. area for long lining life. Hand brake: 8" x 2" spring-loaded drum type mounted on drive line back of transmission. Grip handle on dash.

CLUTCH

Gyro-Grip, easy-action, semi-centrifugal design increases clutch plate pressure with engine speed. 11" diameter 123.7 sq. in. frictional area. Optional: H.D. 11" diameter, 123.7 sq. in. frictional area.

DRIVE LINE

Hotchkiss, straight-line drive. Two tubular propeller shafts with forged steel ends and three highly efficient, long-wearing needle roller bearing universal joints with rubber-encased ball type center bearing.

FRAME

Truck-type with kick-up over rear axle for low loading height. 34" parallel channel side rails: depth 7.0", flange 2.75", thickness 0.21". Section Modulus 5.27. 5-Flanged "U" type cross members.

SHOCK ABSORBERS

Direct, double-acting telescopic design on front, with rubber grommets at mountings.

SPRINGS

Wide-Span, semi-elliptic. Ford alloy steel. Front: 45" by 2", 7 leaves, deflection rate: 338 lbs. per inch. Capacity at pad (normal defl.): 1150 lbs. each. Rear: 52" by 2¼", 8 leaves, deflection rate of 591 lbs. per inch. Capacity at pad (normal defl.): 2400 lbs. each. **Note:** With 8-17.5 6-p.r. front and dual rear tires, optional H.D. 10-leaf, rear springs with 4-leaf auxiliary (at extra cost) are required. Deflection rate: 1313 lbs. per inch, capacity at pad (normal defl.): 3800 lbs. each.

STEERING

Worm and dual row needle bearing roller type with 20.4 to 1 ratio. 3-Spoke, 18" diameter steering wheel. Short-turning circle diameter (left or right): 44.2 ft. Tie rod ball stud and socket type with spring-loaded ends for automatic take-up of wear, equipped with rubber dust shields.

TRANSMISSION

Standard: Easy-Shifting H.D. 3-Speed Synchro-Silent with steering column shift.

Optional (extra cost): Fordomatic with selector lever on steering column or 4-Speed Synchro-Silent with center shift

WHEELS AND TIRES

Five 17.5-inch steel disc with 5.25 rims. Four 8-17.5 6-p.r. tires standard.

Optional: (4) 8-17.5 8-p.r. tires on Std. wheels. (4) 8-19.5 8-p.r. tires on 19.5 x 5.25 wheels. (6) 8-17.6 6-p.r. front and dual rear tires* on std. wheels.

*H.D. rear springs with aux. required.

Comparative information in this folder was obtained from authoritative sources, but is not guaranteed. Ford Truck specifications shown were in effect at time of printing. The Ford Division of Ford Motor Co., whose policy is one of continuous improvement, reserves the right, however, to discontinue models or change at any time, specifications, design or prices without notice and without incurring any obligation. Special equipment, wherever shown, such as special-purpose bodies, is typical of the full range of equipment built by body and equipment manufacturers for use on Ford Trucks. For further information, see your Ford Dealer.

FORD Division of FORD MOTOR COMPANY • DEARBORN, MICHIGAN

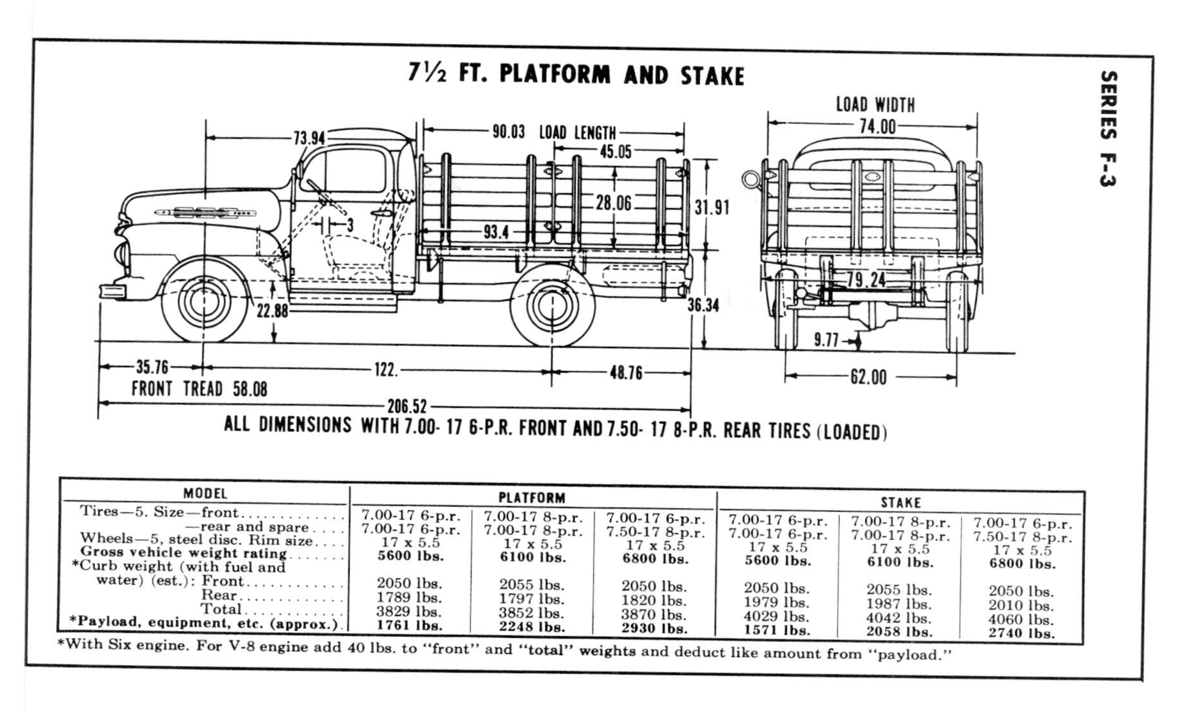

MODEL	PLATFORM			STAKE		
Tires—5. Size—front	7.00-17 6-p.r.	7.00-17 8-p.r.	7.00-17 6-p.r.	7.00-17 6-p.r.	7.00-17 8-p.r.	7.00-17 6-p.r.
—rear and spare	7.00-17 6-p.r.	7.00-17 8-p.r.	7.50-17 8-p.r.	7.00-17 6-p.r.	7.00-17 8-p.r.	7.50-17 8-p.r.
Wheels—5, steel disc. Rim size	17 x 5.5	17 x 5.5	17 x 5.5	17 x 5.5	17 x 5.5	17 x 5.5
Gross vehicle weight rating	**5600 lbs.**	**6100 lbs.**	**6800 lbs.**	**5600 lbs.**	**6100 lbs.**	**6800 lbs.**
*Curb weight (with fuel and water) (est.): Front	2050 lbs.	2055 lbs.	2050 lbs.	2050 lbs.	2055 lbs.	2050 lbs.
Rear	1789 lbs.	1797 lbs.	1820 lbs.	1979 lbs.	1987 lbs.	2010 lbs.
Total	3829 lbs.	3852 lbs.	3870 lbs.	4029 lbs.	4042 lbs.	4060 lbs.
***Payload, equipment, etc. (approx.)**	**1761 lbs.**	**2248 lbs.**	**2930 lbs.**	**1571 lbs.**	**2058 lbs.**	**2740 lbs.**

*With Six engine. For V-8 engine add 40 lbs. to "front" and "**total**" weights and deduct like amount from "payload."

The year is 1951 and a brand-new Diamond T pickup is posed by a larger medium-duty Diamond T wrecker. Applegate & Applegate

clientele (such as those of cleaners and florists). Their expansive, slab-sided exterior panels allowed the buyer to use them as rolling advertisements. The panel also offered purchasers a closed light-duty body that was long (eight feet), wide, roomy, high—and handsome. It was just the ticket for a buyer who needed a distinctive delivery truck to carry large loads with greater ease, safety and security.

Next to the F-1/F-100 pickups, these panels are the most popular Ford commercial vehicles of that era. They are popular now for the same reason they were popular when new: their distinctive looks. Be forewarned, though, that these highly sought after vehicles were produced in far fewer numbers than their pickup-bodied counterparts, so they are not as easy to find. Being more rare will make their value higher in some instances.

To find one of these panels today requires a lot more searching than to find the more common vehicles. But if you want something

Details of this 1955 F-100 panel truck show embossed Ford letters, door handle and door lock.

This 1955 panel makes a nice traveling billboard for Richard's Auto Repair. It's shod with wire wheels and custom tires.

SERIES F-350—9-FT. STAKE AND PLATFORM—130-INCH WB.

CONDENSED SPECIFICATIONS—STANDARD AND OPTIONAL EQUIPMENT
(Refer to UNIT DESIGN Section for more detailed information)

AXLE, FRONT: Modified I-Beam—Capacity (lbs.) 3200
AXLE, REAR: Hypoid, Full Floating—Capacity (lbs.) 7200
Axle ratio with 3- or 4-speed trans.; Std.—5.14 to 1; Opt.—5.83 to 1
Axle ratio with Fordomatic; 5.14 (single rear wheels only)
BODY: Three-piece hinged sides with two-piece end sections (See CABS & BODIES)
BRAKES, SERVICE: Hydraulic—Total lining area (sq. in.) 231
Front—12" x 2"; Rear—13" x 2.5"
BRAKE, HAND: Drum and Contracting Band—Area (sq. in.) 49
CAB: .... 3-man type (See CABS & BODIES)
CLUTCH: .... Semi-Centrifugal, single plate, 11 in. diameter; 123.7 sq. in. area
COOLING SYSTEM:

118-h.p. Six Fans	118-h.p. Six Radiators
Std. 4-Blade, 18" fan (single tires)	Std. 18½ qt. cap'y (with single tires)
4-Blade, 17" fan (dual tires)	
Opt. 5-blade, 17" fan (dual tires)	Opt. 18½ qt. cap'y, H.D. (Req'd on dual tire models; opt. on single tire models)
132-h.p. V-8 Fans	**132-h.p. V-8 Radiators**
Std. 4-blade, 18" fan	Std. 22 qt. cap'y (with single tires)
Opt. 5-blade, 18" fan (dual tire models only)	Opt. 22 qt. cap'y, H.D. (Req'd on dual tire models, opt. on single tire models)

DRIVE LINE: .... Two tubular shafts with three needle bearing universal joints
ELECTRICAL: 6 volt, 17 plate, 90 amp-hr. battery; 35 amp, 250 watt generator; parking lights; l.h. stop and tail light; sealed beam headlights with foot switch beam control; push button starter switch; single horn.
ENGINES:

	Cost Clipper Six	Power King V-8
Displacement—cu. in.	223	239
Max. Brake Horsepower @ RPM	118 @ 3800	132 @ 4200
Max. Torque—Lbs.-Ft. @ RPM	195 @ 1200-2400	215 @ 1800-2200
Compression Ratio	7.5 to 1	7.5 to 1

Full pressure lubrication, oil filter (optional), 1 qt. oil bath air cleaner, Power Pilot carburetion-ignition.
FRAME: .... Parallel channel side rails with 5 cross members;
Max. side rail section—7.0" x 2.75" x .212"; Section Modulus—5.27
FUEL TANK: .... Below cab, outside left frame rail; 17 gallon capacity
PAINT: .... (See CABS & BODIES)
SHOCK ABSORBERS: Front .... Direct, Double Acting, Telescopic
SPRINGS: .... Semi-Elliptic, leaf-type
Standard—Front—7 leaf, 45" x 2"; Rear—8 leaf, 52" x 2¼"
Optional rear main—10 leaf, 52" x 2¼"
Optional rear aux.—4 leaf, 37" x 2¼" (dual rear tire models only)
STEERING: ...... Worm and Roller; 20.4 to 1 ratio; 18 in. diameter steering wheel
TRANSMISSION: Std.—3-speed H.D., Synchro-Silent, steering column shift
Opt.—4-speed Synchro-Silent, center shift
Opt.—Fordomatic (up thru 7700 lbs. G.V.W.) with single rear wheels only
WHEELS & TIRES: Standard—Five 17 x 5.50 wheels with four 7.00-17 6-p.r. tires
Optional—Five standard wheels with four 7.00-17 8-p.r. tires or four 7.50-17 8-p.r. tires
Optional—Five standard wheels with two 7.00-17 6-p.r. tires (front) and two 7.50-17 8-p.r. tires (rear)
Optional—Seven 16 x 5.50F wheels with six 7.50-16 6-p.r. tires*
*Heavy duty rear springs mandatory
MISCELLANEOUS STANDARD EQUIPMENT WITH CAB: channel front bumper . . . short running boards . . . tire carrier under platform . . . l.h. sun visor . . . l.h. outside mirror . . . dual windshield wipers . . . hand throttle . . . jack and tools . . . center cowl ventilator . . . ash receptacle . . . dispatch box.
(For optional equipment, see page FSM-32)

More dimensions and specifications of the alternative chassis and body styles for 1955.

a little more special, your extra efforts will be rewarded. One tip is that these vehicles were popular with the surfing crowd in the sixties, so you may want to start your search in the beach areas of California. Good luck.

SERIES F-350 CHASSIS WITH CAB—130-INCH WB.

CONDENSED SPECIFICATIONS—STANDARD AND OPTIONAL EQUIPMENT
(Refer to UNIT DESIGN Section for more detailed information)

AXLE, FRONT: Modified I-Beam—Capacity (lbs.)........................3200
AXLE, REAR: Hypoid, Full Floating—Capacity (lbs.).....................7200
Axle ratio with 3- or 4-speed trans.; Std.—5.14 to 1; Opt. 5.83 to 1.
Axle ratio with Fordomatic; 5.14 (single rear wheels only)
BRAKES, SERVICE: Hydraulic—Total lining area (sq. in.)...................231
Front—12" x 2"; Rear—13" x 2.5"
BRAKE, HAND: Drum and Contracting Band—Area (sq. in.)................49
CAB:..................................3-man type (See CABS & BODIES)
CLUTCH:........Semi-Centrifugal, single plate, 11 in. diameter; 123.7 sq. in. area
COOLING SYSTEM:

118-h.p. Six Fans	118-h.p. Six Radiators
Std. 4-Blade, 18" fan (single tires)	Std. 18½ qt. cap'y (with single tires)
4-Blade, 17" fan (dual tires)	
Opt. 5-blade, 17" diam. fan (dual tires)	Opt. 18½ qt. cap'y, H.D. (Req'd on dual tire models, opt. on single tire models)
132-h.p. V-8 Fans	132-h.p. V-8 Radiators
Std. 4-blade, 18" diam. fan	Std. 22 qt. cap'y (with single tires)
Opt. 5-blade, 18" fan (dual tire models only)	Opt. 22 qt. cap'y. H.D. (Req'd on dual tire models, opt. on single tire models)

DRIVE LINE:.......Two tubular shafts with three needle bearing universal joints
ELECTRICAL: 6 volt, 17 plate, 90 amp-hr. battery; 35 amp, 250 watt generator; parking lights; l.h. stop and tail light; sealed beam headlights with foot switch beam control; push button starter switch; single horn.
ENGINES:

	Cost Clipper Six	Power King V-8
Displacement—cu. in.	223	239
Max. Brake Horsepower @ RPM	118 @ 3800	132 @ 4200
Max. Torque—Lbs.-Ft. @ RPM	195 @ 1200-2400	215 @ 1800-2200
Compression Ratio	7.5 to 1	7.5 to 1

Full pressure lubrication, oil filter (optional), 1 qt. oil bath air cleaner, Power Pilot carburetion-ignition.
FRAME:.......................Parallel channel side rails with 5 cross members; Max. side rail section—7.0" x 2.75" x .212"; Section Modulus—5.27
FUEL TANK:..............Below cab, outside left frame rail; 17 gallon capacity
PAINT:..(See CABS & BODIES)
SHOCK ABSORBERS: Front.................Direct, Double Acting, Telescopic
SPRINGS:...Semi-Elliptic, leaf-type
Standard—Front—7 leaf, 45" x 2"; Rear—8 leaf, 52" x 2¼"
Optional rear main—10 leaf, 52" x 2¼"
Optional rear aux.—4 leaf, 37" x 2¼" (dual rear tire models only)
STEERING:......Worm and Roller; 20.4 to 1 ratio; 18 in. diameter steering wheel
TRANSMISSION: Std.—3-speed H.D., Synchro-Silent, steering column shift
Opt.—4-speed Synchro-Silent, center shift
Opt.—Fordomatic (up thru 7700 lbs. G.V.W.) single rear wheels only
WHEELS & TIRES: Standard—Five 17 x 5.50 wheels with four 7.00-17 6-p.r. tires
Optional—Five standard wheels with four 7.00-17 8-p.r. tires or four 7.50-17 8-p.r. tires
Optional—Five standard wheels with two 7.00-17 6-p.r. tires (front) and two 7.50-17 8-p.r. tires (rear)
Optional—Seven 16 x 5.50F wheels with six 7.50-16 6-p.r. tires*
*Heavy duty rear springs mandatory
MISCELLANEOUS STANDARD EQUIPMENT WITH CAB: channel front bumper . . . short running boards . . . tire carrier under frame . . . l.h. sun visor . . . l.h. outside mirror . . . dual windshield wipers . . . hand throttle . . . jack and tools . . . center cowl ventilator . . . ash receptacle . . . dispatch box.

(For optional equipment, see page FSM-32)

SERIES F-100 8-FT. PANEL—110-INCH WB.

CONDENSED SPECIFICATIONS—STANDARD AND OPTIONAL EQUIPMENT
(Refer to UNIT DESIGN Section for more detailed information)

AXLE, FRONT: Modified I-Beam—Capacity (lbs.)........................2600
AXLE, REAR: Hypoid, Semi-Floating—Capacity (lbs.)....................3300
Axle ratio with 3- or 4-speed trans.; Std.—3.92 to 1; Opt.—4.27 to 1
Axle ratio with Overdrive trans.; Std.—4.09 to 1; Opt.—4.27 to 1
Axle ratio with Fordomatic trans.; Std.—3.92 to 1
BODY:.......................Reinforced welded steel (See CABS & BODIES)
BRAKES, SERVICE: Hydraulic—Total lining area (sq. in.)...................179
Front—11" x 2"; Rear—11" x 1¾". Optional—Vacuum Booster
BRAKE, HAND:..............Cable with Equalizer applying Rear Wheel Brakes
CLUTCH:......................................Semi-Centrifugal, single plate
Standard—10 in. diameter; 85.5 sq. in. frictional area
COOLING SYSTEM:

	Standard	Optional
118-h.p. Six:	18½ qt. cap'y—4-blade, 18" diam. fan	H. D. radiator
132-h.p. V-8:	22 qt. cap'y—4-blade, 18" diam. fan	H. D. radiator

DRIVE LINE:..........One tubular shaft with two needle bearing universal joints
ELECTRICAL:....6 volt, 17 plate, 90 amp.-hr. battery; 35 amp., 250 watt generator; parking lights; two stop and tail lights; sealed beam headlights with foot switch beam control; push-button starter switch; single horn.
ENGINES:

	Cost Clipper Six	Power King V-8
Displacement—cu. in.	223	239
Max. Brake Horsepower @ RPM	118 @ 3800	132 @ 4200
Max. Torque—Lbs.-Ft. @ RPM	195 @ 1200-2400	215 @ 1800-2200
Compression Ratio	7.5 to 1	7.5 to 1

Full pressure lubrication, oil filter (optional), 1 qt. oil bath air cleaner, Power Pilot carburetion-ignition.
FRAME:.......................Parallel channel side rails with 4 cross members
Max. side rail section—5.92" x 2.25" x 0.15"; Section Modulus—2.65
FUEL TANK:.....................Inside left frame rail; 17 gallon capacity
PAINT:..(See CABS & BODIES)
SHOCK ABSORBERS: Front and rear;..........Direct, Double Acting, Telescopic
SPRINGS:...Semi-Elliptic, leaf type
Standard—Front—8 leaf, 42" x 1¾"; Rear—6 leaf, 52" x 2"
Optional—H.D. Two-stage rear main—9 leaf, 52" x 2"
STEERING:......Worm and Roller; 18.2 to 1 ratio; 18 in. diameter steering wheel
TRANSMISSION: Std.—3-speed Synchro-Silent, steering column shift.
Opt.—3-speed H.D., Synchro-Silent, steering column shift.
Opt.—4-speed, Synchro-Silent, center shift.
Opt.—3-speed, with Overdrive.
Opt.—Fordomatic
WHEELS & TIRES:......Standard—16 x 4½ K wheels with five 6.00-16 6-p.r. tires
Optional—Standard wheels with five 6.00-16 4-p.r. or 6.50-16 6-p.r. tires
MISCELLANEOUS STANDARD EQUIPMENT: channel front and rear bumpers . . . long running boards . . . hub caps . . . tire carrier under frame . . . l.h. sun visor . . . l.h. outside mirror . . . dual w/s wipers . . . jack and tools . . . center cowl ventilator . . . ash receptacle . . . dispatch box.

(For optional equipment, see page FSM—12)

6½-FT. PLATFORM AND STAKE

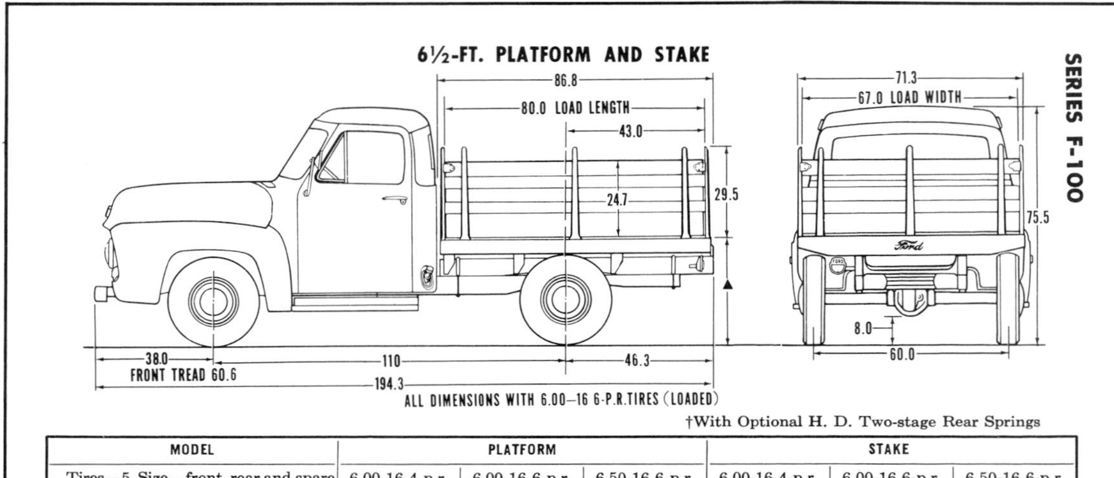

†With Optional H. D. Two-stage Rear Springs

MODEL	PLATFORM			STAKE		
Tires—5, Size—front, rear and spare	6.00-16 4-p.r.	6.00-16 6-p.r.	6.50-16 6-p.r.	6.00-16 4-p.r.	6.00-16 6-p.r.	6.50-16 6-p.r.
Wheels—5, steel disc. Rim size	16 x 4½K	16 x 4½K	16 x 4½K	16 x 4½K	16 x 4½K	16 x 4½K
▲Loaded rear height	**32.8 in.**	**32.8 in.**	**32.9 in.**	**32.8 in.**	**32.8 in.**	**32.9 in.**
Gross vehicle weight rating	**4000 lbs.**	**4400 lbs.**	**5000 lbs.†**	**4000 lbs.**	**4400 lbs.**	**5000 lbs.†**
*Curb weight (est.) (with fuel and water)						
Front	1980 lbs.	1984 lbs.	1992 lbs.	1990 lbs.	1994 lbs.	2002 lbs.
Rear	1200 lbs.	1206 lbs.	1250 lbs.	1315 lbs.	1321 lbs.	1365 lbs.
Total	3180 lbs.	3190 lbs.	3242 lbs.	3305 lbs.	3315 lbs.	3367 lbs.
***Payload, equipment, etc. (approx.)**	**820 lbs.**	**1210 lbs.**	**1758 lbs.**	**695 lbs.**	**1085 lbs.**	**1633 lbs.**

*With Six engine. For V-8 engine add 100 lbs. to "front" and "total" weights and deduct like amount from "payload."

8-FT. PANEL

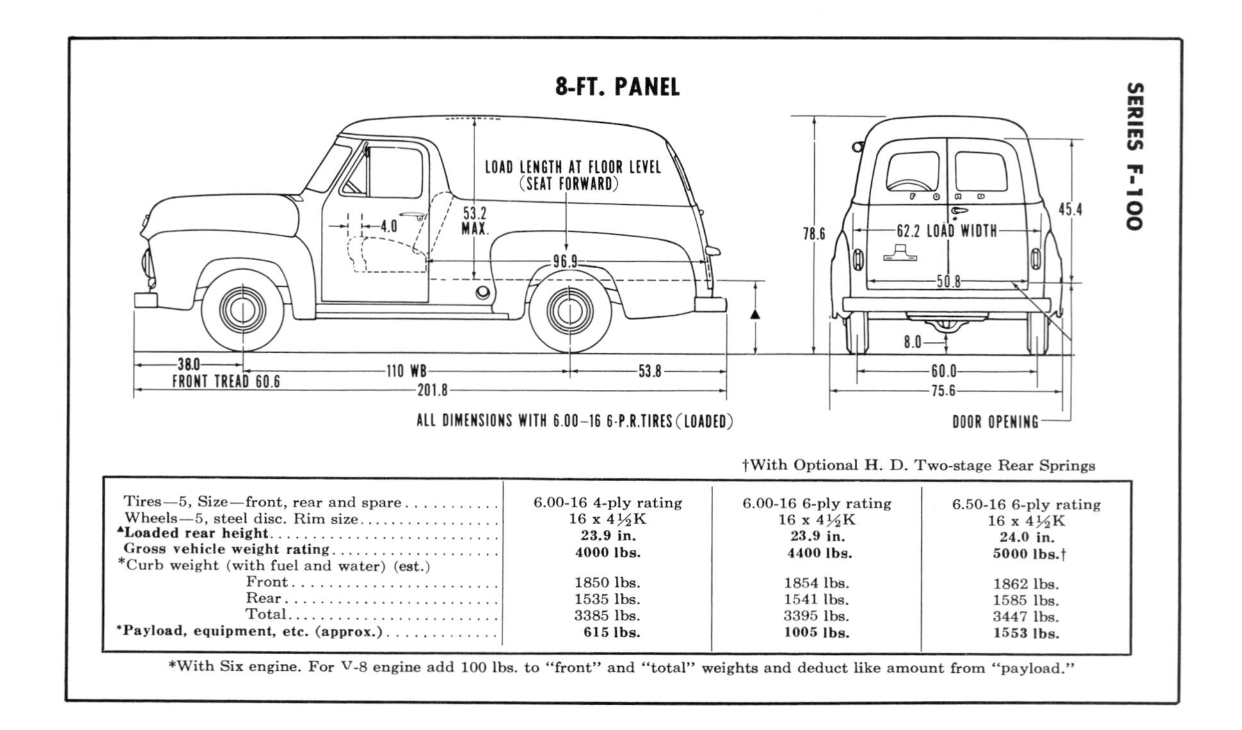

†With Optional H. D. Two-stage Rear Springs

Tires—5, Size—front, rear and spare	6.00-16 4-ply rating	6.00-16 6-ply rating	6.50-16 6-ply rating
Wheels—5, steel disc. Rim size	16 x 4½K	16 x 4½K	16 x 4½K
▲Loaded rear height	**23.9 in.**	**23.9 in.**	**24.0 in.**
Gross vehicle weight rating	**4000 lbs.**	**4400 lbs.**	**5000 lbs.†**
*Curb weight (with fuel and water) (est.)			
Front	1850 lbs.	1854 lbs.	1862 lbs.
Rear	1535 lbs.	1541 lbs.	1585 lbs.
Total	3385 lbs.	3395 lbs.	3447 lbs.
***Payload, equipment, etc. (approx.)**	**615 lbs.**	**1005 lbs.**	**1553 lbs.**

*With Six engine. For V-8 engine add 100 lbs. to "front" and "total" weights and deduct like amount from "payload."

CHASSIS WITH CAB

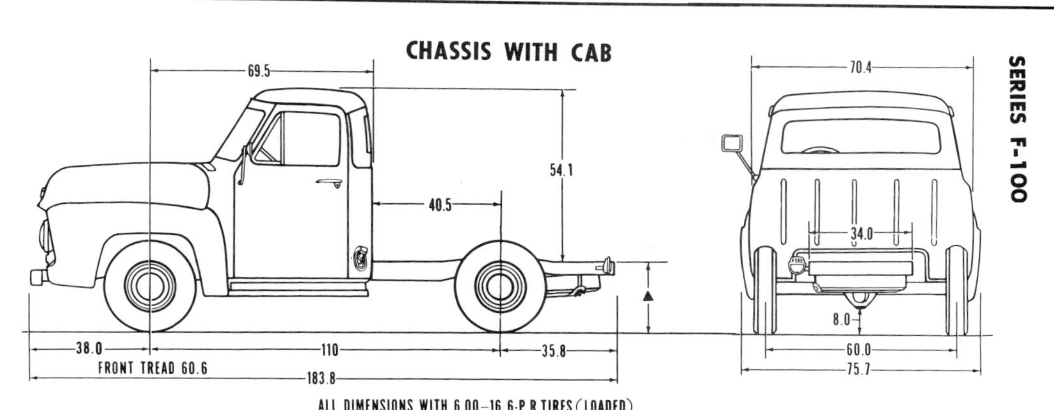

ALL DIMENSIONS WITH 6.00–16 6-P.R. TIRES (LOADED)

†With Optional H. D. Two-stage Rear Springs

Tires—5, Size—front, rear and spare	6.00-16 4-ply rating	6.00-16 6-ply rating	6.50-16 6-ply rating
Wheels—5, steel disc. Rim size	16 x 4½K	16 x 4½K	16 x 4½K
▲**Loaded rear height**	**21.3 in.**	**21.3 in.**	**21.4 in.**
Gross vehicle weight rating	**4000 lbs.**	**4400 lbs.**	**5000 lbs.†**
*Curb weight (with fuel and water) (est.)			
Front	1980 lbs.	1984 lbs.	1992 lbs.
Rear	890 lbs.	896 lbs.	940 lbs.
Total	2870 lbs.	2880 lbs.	2932 lbs.
***Payload, body, equipment, etc. (approx.)**	**1130 lbs.**	**1520 lbs.**	**2068 lbs.**

*With Six engine. For V-8 engine add 100 lbs. to "front" and "total" weights and deduct like amount from "payload."

CHASSIS WITH COWL

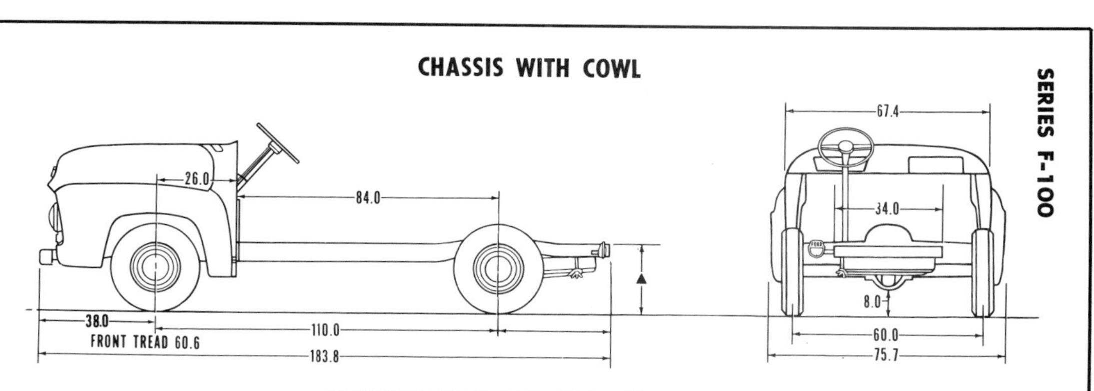

ALL DIMENSIONS WITH 6.00–16 6-P.R. TIRES (LOADED)

†With Optional H. D. Two-stage Rear Springs

MODEL	CHASSIS WITH COWL		
Tires—5, Size—front, rear and spare	6.00-16 4-ply rating	6.00-16 6-ply rating	6.50-16 6-ply rating
Wheels—5, steel disc. Rim size	16 x 4½K	16 x 4½K	16 x 4½K
▲**Loaded rear height**	**21.3 in.**	**21.3 in.**	**21.4 in.**
Gross vehicle weight rating	**4000 lbs.**	**4400 lbs.**	**5000 lbs.†**
*Curb weight (est.) (with fuel and water)			
Front	1665 lbs.	1669 lbs.	1677 lbs.
Rear	705 lbs.	711 lbs.	755 lbs.
Total	2370 lbs.	2380 lbs.	2432 lbs.
***Payload, body, equipment, etc. (approx.)**	**1630 lbs.**	**2020 lbs.**	**2568 lbs.**

*With Six engine. For V-8 engine add 100 lbs. to "front" and "total" weights and deduct like amount from "payload."

This 1956 has custom wheels and tires.

Note the sculpturing in panels and special 1941 Ford fender panels on this 1956 panel truck body. These panels are much narrower than on a pickup.

This rear-end shot of two 1956 F-100 panel trucks shows rear door, license-plate mount and taillight details. The open doors show that the owner had a custom diamond-pattern velour interior installed.

Helping to dress up this 1956 F-100 panel truck are chromed grille, custom wheels and tires, window bright trim and fuzzy dice hanging from the mirror.

Custom wheels and tires help to dress up this 1956 panel truck, as seen at the 1985 North/South Run in Fresno, California.

A 390 ci FE big-block V-8 powers this modified F-350 1956 owned by Rick Louderbough of New Mexico.

Gare Perry of New Mexico owns this flamed, custom 1956 panel. Inside, a full custom interior is featured—a real crowd pleaser on the show circuit.

The custom features of this modified panel truck really make it stand out in a crowd! It has lowered springs, custom wheels and tires, and a custom flame paint job, to name a few.

Chrome running board and custom wheels and tires on this modified panel set it apart.

Chapter 4

Restoring the glow to that diamond in the rough

The visual inspection

So you went out and did it; you found that fifties Ford pickup of your dreams and hauled it back home. What are you going to do with it now? Where do you start? Now is the time to take stock of the situation, to see how much work is needed to turn this frog back into a prince.

First, get a loose-leaf binder with lots of paper and a set of dividers. On the first page, make a checklist of all the items that are going to need attention. Divide these areas into five major categories and mark the dividers accordingly: Mechanical, Body, Frame, Interior, Electrical. By dividing your information into groups, you'll be able to keep track of your note taking in an orderly fashion. Then if you have to refer back to the book at a later date, it will be much easier to use.

Before you bought your truck, you should have taken a test drive in it and made mental notes about how the major components

Fred Martin of Massachusetts owns this 1950 F-1.

worked. Was the engine sluggish? Did it use oil? Did the transmission shift easily, or did it seem hard to get through the gears? Did it stop as it should? Did it seem to shimmy a little as you drove? The answers to these questions will give you a general idea of what shape the vehicle is in. All your impressions of how well it runs should be put in the Mechanical section of your binder.

Next comes the visual inspection. The first area under scrutiny should be the body and its related parts. This will include the cab proper, the front-end sheet metal and the bed. Make notes about the paint, missing trim and damaged areas of the body, both those that have been fixed and those that haven't. (Here, I mean areas that have seen the bondo palette but the repair may not have been done properly.) You may want to carry a marking pencil to highlight the areas that require work.

While you are at it, check for rust-outs; these trucks are not immune from the ravages of rot. (Keep in mind that your truck was probably a real workhorse and nobody had the time or inclination to make sure it was cleaned off properly after being subjected to areas and conditions that allow rust and rot to thrive.) Surface rust can be a minor irritant, but rust-outs can cause major problems. These trucks were known to rust out in the corner areas, inside the fenders, on the floorboards, on the bottoms of the doors, in the frame rails, and sometimes on the roof near the rain gutters and around the windshield. Some rust problems have also surfaced inside the cowls. (When you do the underside inspection you can also check for rust areas.)

After the cab body and front end have been checked, it's time to look the bed over. Most of these trucks had hardwood floors,

Past this lineup of 1956 models with the Big Window feature stands a 1953 in the background.

and the wood should be showing its age. In some cases you may see more undercarriage than hardwood. But don't despair; kits are available that will make the bed floor look better than new. Also check the tailgate for proper operation and fit.

Make sure the hood opens and closes without any problems. The hood hinges on Ford trucks of this era had a tendency to bind up, especially on the 1953-56 models. If this problem is not attended to, one runs the risk of damaging the hood or, worse yet, the cowl area. Take care of this problem first, and attend to the others later.

With your exterior inspection complete now you can put your glad rags on and take a look underneath. But first, if your undercarriage area is full of grease and grime, a trip to the local, hand-held, high-powered car wash is in order. Just blast away underneath; a cleaner vehicle will be easier to check and will also be more appealing to work on. Usually the cleaner the car the better the repair work.

Now you can make a thorough inspection. Start at the front of the vehicle and work your way back. With the vehicle safely supported off the ground, check the front end on both sides to make sure everything is tight and in good working order. If you suspect that anything is amiss or that the front end hasn't been worked on in a while, you might as well figure on replacing the king pins and related hardware. (This is especially true if you plan on running wider wheels and tires.) Also check the steering gear and components; if there is any play, plan on replacing or rebuild-

This close-up of a 1953 headlight shows its fine details.

Front fenders of 1953 models were certainly bulbous.

ing pieces. While you are in the area, check the brakes and brake lines for leaks and worn-out components. If the rest of the front end needs work, you can also expect that the springs and shocks will need to be repaired or replaced. Front-end work can be expensive but this is an area that you shouldn't scrimp on; if everything works properly, you'll have a safer and more enjoyable vehicle to drive.

As you work back, check for leaks coming from the oil pan, transmission case and rear end. Also check the frame for cracks and rust damage, especially around the cross-member areas. This is critical if your truck has had an engine or transmission transplant, since some owners have unwisely removed cross-members and their supports to provide extra clearance. If your truck's chassis has been modified in this manner, don't despair; new cross-members can be installed to add that much needed rigidity to the frame.

Check the exhaust system and plan on replacing parts here, too. If you need to rework the front end then it's a sure bet the back end will need some looking after too. If the springs seem to be sagging, a trip to a spring shop is in order, or maybe a new set is more to your liking. After this inspection, your budget is going to start getting strained, but then again nobody ever said the restoration business was going to be easy or cheap.

Now it's time to concentrate on the inside of the cab. If you are lucky, your pride and joy won't need too much work in this area, but if it does, don't worry; practically everything you see can be replaced with new parts—everything from gauges to seat covers to headliners. Armrests, door panels, sun visors and trim items can be bought from the parts specialists listed elsewhere in this book. All you need is some cash!

The last area of concern is the electrical system and associated wiring. Check this area completely by testing all gauges and electrical equipment and by visually inspecting the wiring from stem to stern. Some of these trucks feature "rat's nests" for wiring. If your truck suffers from such a malady, new harnesses will take care of any problems.

With your electrical system check done, your visual check is complete. While you were doing your checking, I hope you remembered to jot everything down. If you did, your notes will give you a good idea as to

This 1955 "work" truck has custom wheels and tires, perhaps not what you'd call pretty but it gets the job done.

A local telephone company used this 1955 model, and it remains stock as it was then.

the amount of work you'll need to do to complete this restoration. You'll also have a list of items that need attention, and you should prioritize it so that critical items are taken care of first. Your notes will also tell you how extensive the overall job will be. If you are lucky, a simple or cosmetic restoration is all that is needed; if you are unlucky, a complete overhaul is in order. Most of the time, the job will fall somewhere in between. With your notebook in hand you can sit down and start planning your project.

This 1955 standard cab has the regular-size rear window.

Custom wheels and tires, 302 Ford V-8 under hood and Detroit Locker rear end adorn this 1956 F-100 owned by Joe Abbin of New Mexico.

Getting down to brass tacks

After doing a visual inspection and reading over the notes in your book, you now have a good idea of how much work your vehicle is going to need. If paint and minor body work are all that is required then your job won't be that hard. If an interior restoration and/or bed restoration is needed, you are still on easy street. But if everything needs work then you are probably looking at a frame-up restoration, which will require considerably more time, more money and more effort. If you are facing that type of situation, don't throw the towel in yet because most of the work needed

This 1956 has received the full custom treatment: paint, wheels, tires, Chevelle front clip, blown 302 Ford engine.

This modified 1956 model was found at the North/South Run in Fresno, California, in 1985.

to refurbish these vehicles is well within the capabilities of anyone who can use simple hand tools. Most of the major components unbolt from the structure, greatly easing the chore.

To do the job right, you'll need plenty of room to disassemble the vehicle and to work on it. You'll need the usual tools plus jack stands, a hydraulic jack, some sawhorses and storage room for the pieces you remove. If you are planning to remove the engine, transmission or rear end, you'll also need some specialized tools.

Before you start be sure you have plenty of paper in your notebook for drawings and notes, and a camera and film for taking pictures. It's also a good idea to have some marking pencils, coffee cans, bags, boxes and so on to store the nuts, bolts and such that you remove. As you remove a part and its attachments, you can place them in a container and identify them (such as, bolts—left front fender). When it comes time to reassemble items, you'll have a much easier job. The more time you spend disassembling the vehicle, the faster it will go back together.

Now that you have everything ready, you can disassemble your truck. Start with the easy items, like wheels and tires (unless you plan on moving the vehicle once you start). Make sure the vehicle is supported on steady jack stands or other equipment made for this purpose. Don't lift the vehicle too high, just high enough so you can move underneath comfortably.

Next on the agenda is the bed removal or the front-end sheet metal removal. (If your truck doesn't need the work covered in this or another area, pass over it.) If you start with the bed, its removal is pretty easy: Just get under the truck and unbolt it from the frame. You may want to unbolt the fenders and tailgate first, before you remove the bed, thereby making the piece a little lighter. (You may need a couple of friends to help you with the lifting.) After you remove the bed, support it across some sawhorses so you can more comfortably work on it at waist level. (Saw horses can be used for working on all major components that require a flat working surface. If you need a table, add a piece of plywood.)

The brightwork, vent window and mirror mounting have been eliminated on this 1956 F-100 standard cab. Owner has also added a custom interior.

Wide custom wheels and tires, tonneau cover snaps, antique taillights and chromed running board strips are some of the highlights on this 1956 F-100.

With the bed off the truck, you can replace and/or repair what needs to be done before you disassemble any other part of your truck. This type of subassembly restoration has a lot of merit to it. Concentrating on one part at a time reduces the tendency to become overwhelmed by the enormity of the project. If you are like most people, your stamina and determination may fail before you can complete a total restoration. Burnout sets in and most people give up on the project. However, if you complete the restoration of each subassembly individually, you'll find that the glamor and fun of the job will last a lot longer.

Once you have refurbished the bed, it's time to remove all the front-end components forward of the cowl area. The first thing to come off is the hood (here again you will need the help of your friends). Once the hood is out of the way, you can get to all the bolts and fasteners that hold the fenders, inner panels, grille and other components in place. If your drivetrain needs work, this is a good time to pull it; with the front end bare, the job is a lot easier.

If you don't plan on removing the body, now would be a good time to concentrate on cleaning up the front portion of the frame. You can remove items, clean and degrease them, repaint and refurbish them, and then reinstall them. With all the components removed from the frame, you can paint it with Ford Chassis Black to give your restoration the factory look. Remember to prepare the surface properly and take the time to do the job neatly. (By the way, when Ford origi-

Big Window option on a 1956 Custom Cab. This feature is more in demand because it's more rare than the regular window.

Pinstriping patterns can be as varied as the personalities of the owners. One example is shown on this 1956.

Pinstriping is a nice touch to this 1956. The fenderline is very bulbous.

The owner of this 1956 F-100 Big Window customized the truck to include a lowered front, by using a dropped front axle (a popular fifties touch). There are also custom wheels and tires and a chromed differential cover. The back end features a tailgate on the pickup box that was taken from an earlier vintage Ford truck. On top of the bed is a custom-fitted tonneau cover. Note the club plaque in the back window, a nice period piece.

nally built those frames they weren't spray painted, they were dipped in the paint to make sure they got a good, thick, uniform covering. It was hoped that this coating would be more chip resistant and better able to withstand the rigors of truck use.)

The last item to come off should be the body itself. This is another simple unbolting procedure; that is, it is simple after the interior has been stripped. (Once again, removal of the body will require the help of friends.) With everything removed, including the body, you'll have an easier time cleaning and repairing the frame.

After the frame work has been completed, you can begin reassembling the truck—just reverse the disassembly procedure. When you get to the point of reinstalling the interior, glass and trim, I suggest you prepare and repaint the exterior first.

Restoring one of these beauties is a pretty straightforward project. My best advice is to take your time and make sure everything is as it should be before moving on to the next step. No matter how you go about performing any of the steps, the important thing to keep in mind is not to rush the project.

The difficult factor, if there is one, will depend on the amount of work needed and the skill level of the restorer. If you are a veteran you won't find the job too tough, and if you are new at this restoration game, I can't think of a better project to cut your teeth on.

What could be better to a Ford truck enthusiast than a parking lot full of 1956 F-100s?

This 1956 street rodder has custom wheels and tires, Chevy V-8, no hood.

This 1955 is mostly stock with the minor changes of custom wheels and tires.

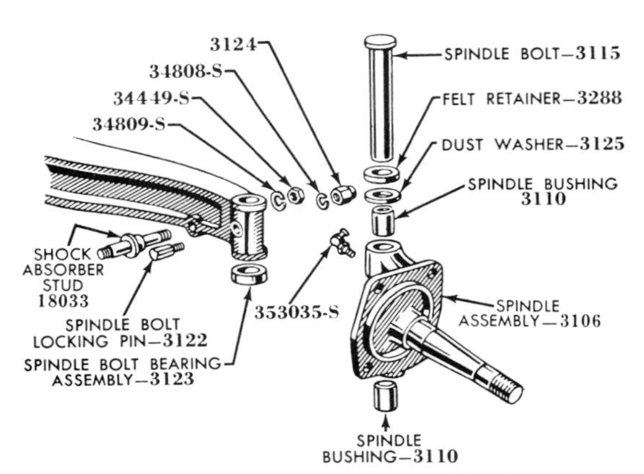

A typical front axle spindle assembly. This is an early 1950s drawing but will apply to all vehicles covered in this book.

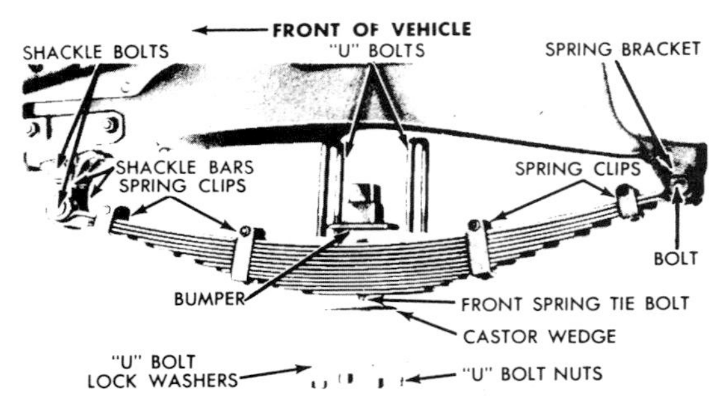

Front spring assemblies are again similar throughout all truck models.

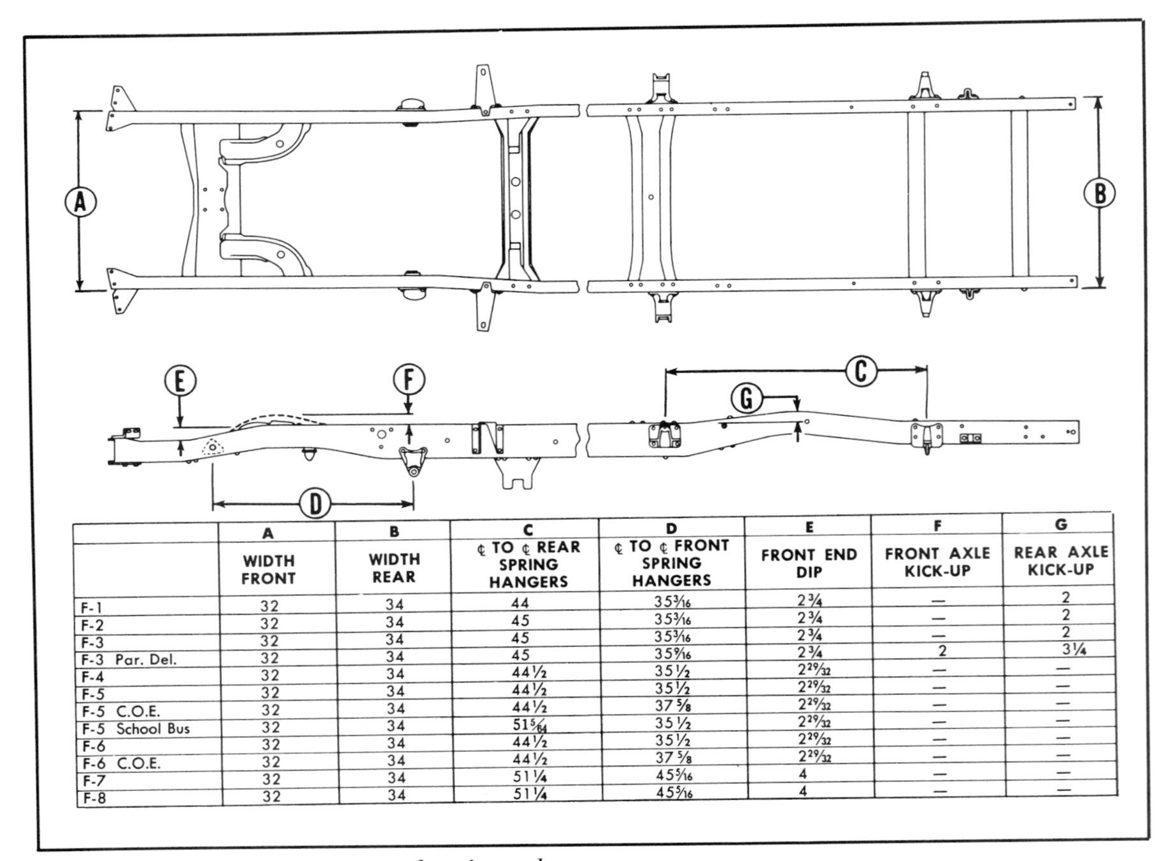

	A	B	C	D	E	F	G
	WIDTH FRONT	WIDTH REAR	¢ TO ¢ REAR SPRING HANGERS	¢ TO ¢ FRONT SPRING HANGERS	FRONT END DIP	FRONT AXLE KICK-UP	REAR AXLE KICK-UP
F-1	32	34	44	35 3/16	2 3/4	—	2
F-2	32	34	45	35 3/16	2 3/4	—	2
F-3	32	34	45	35 3/16	2 3/4	—	2
F-3 Par. Del.	32	34	45	35 9/16	2 3/4	2	3 1/4
F-4	32	34	44 1/2	35 1/2	2 29/32	—	—
F-5	32	34	44 1/2	35 1/2	2 29/32	—	—
F-5 C.O.E.	32	34	44 1/2	37 5/8	2 29/32	—	—
F-5 School Bus	32	34	51 5/64	35 1/2	2 29/32	—	—
F-6	32	34	44 1/2	35 1/2	2 29/32	—	—
F-6 C.O.E.	32	34	44 1/2	37 5/8	2 29/32	—	—
F-7	32	34	51 1/4	45 5/16	4	—	—
F-8	32	34	51 1/4	45 5/16	4	—	—

Truck chassis frame dimensions taken from the factory manual for the years 1949-51.

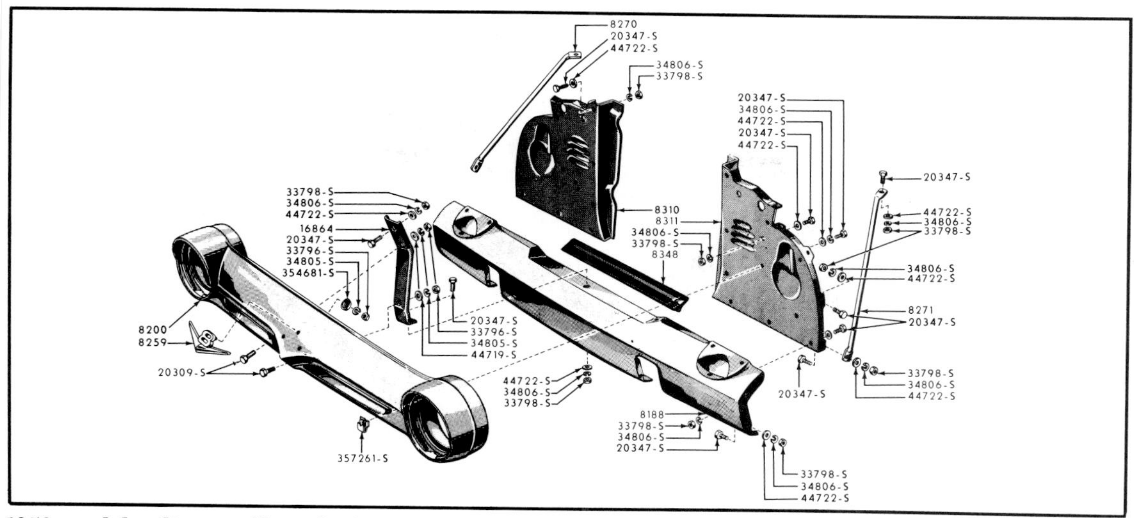

1956 model radiator grille and related parts of the "conventional" cab version.

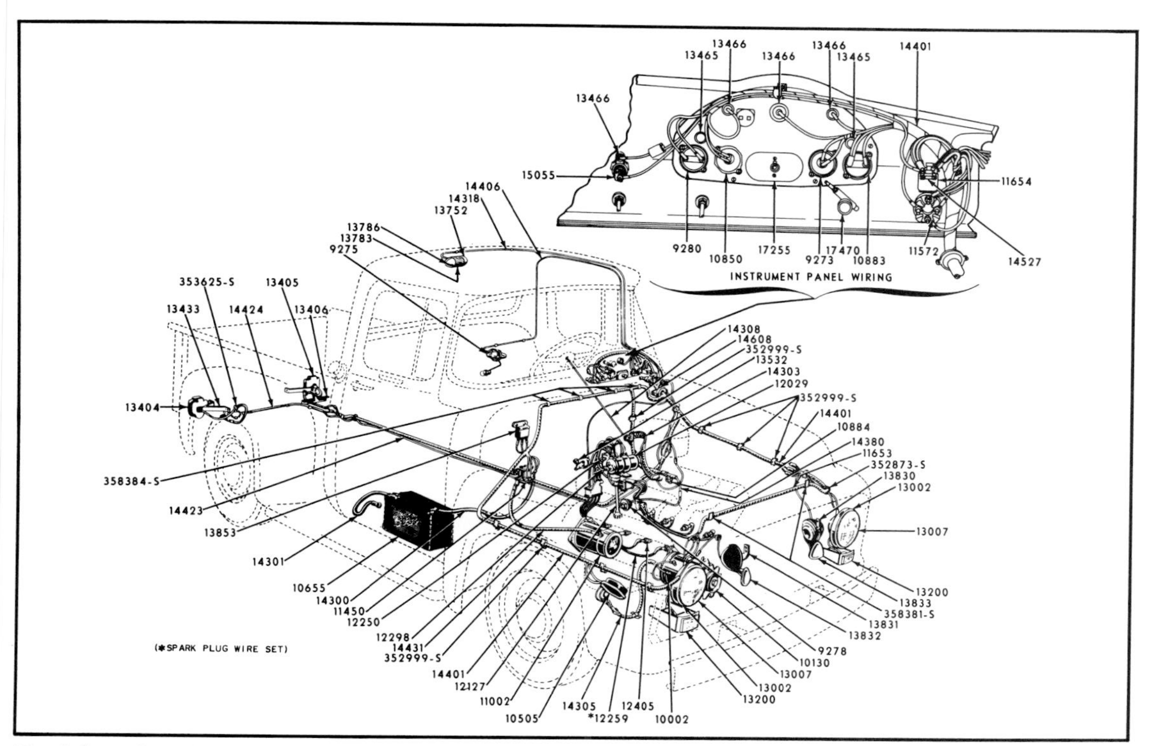

Ford describes this as a typical wiring loom (in its October 1955 parts list). Nice outline of a 1956 step-side.

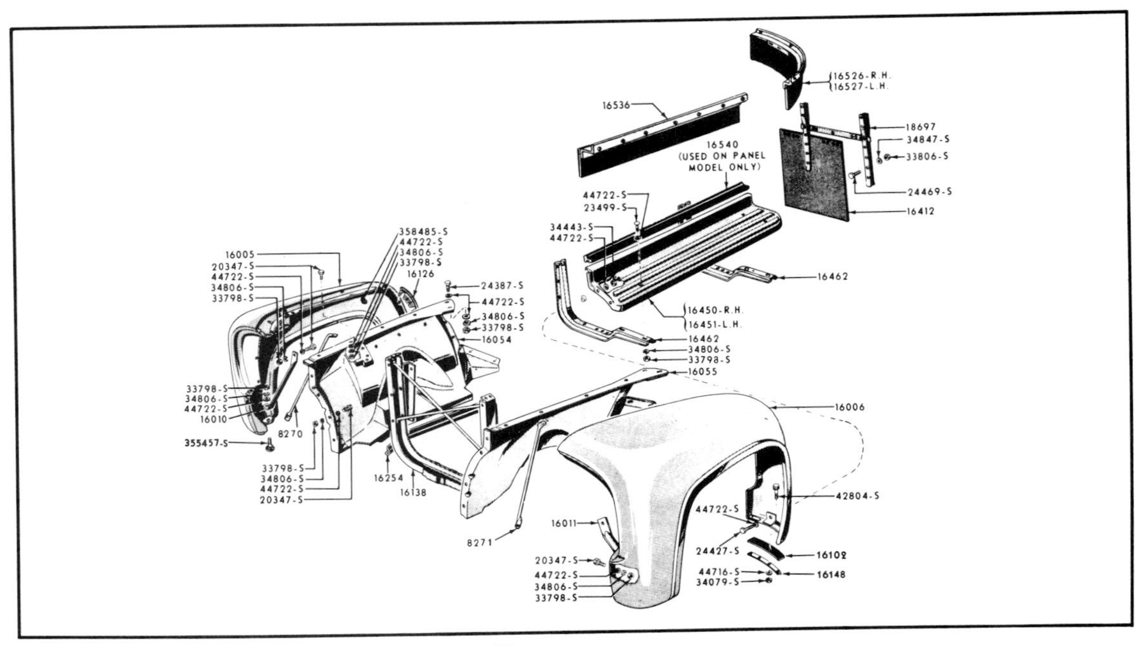

Late-model fender and running board assemblies.

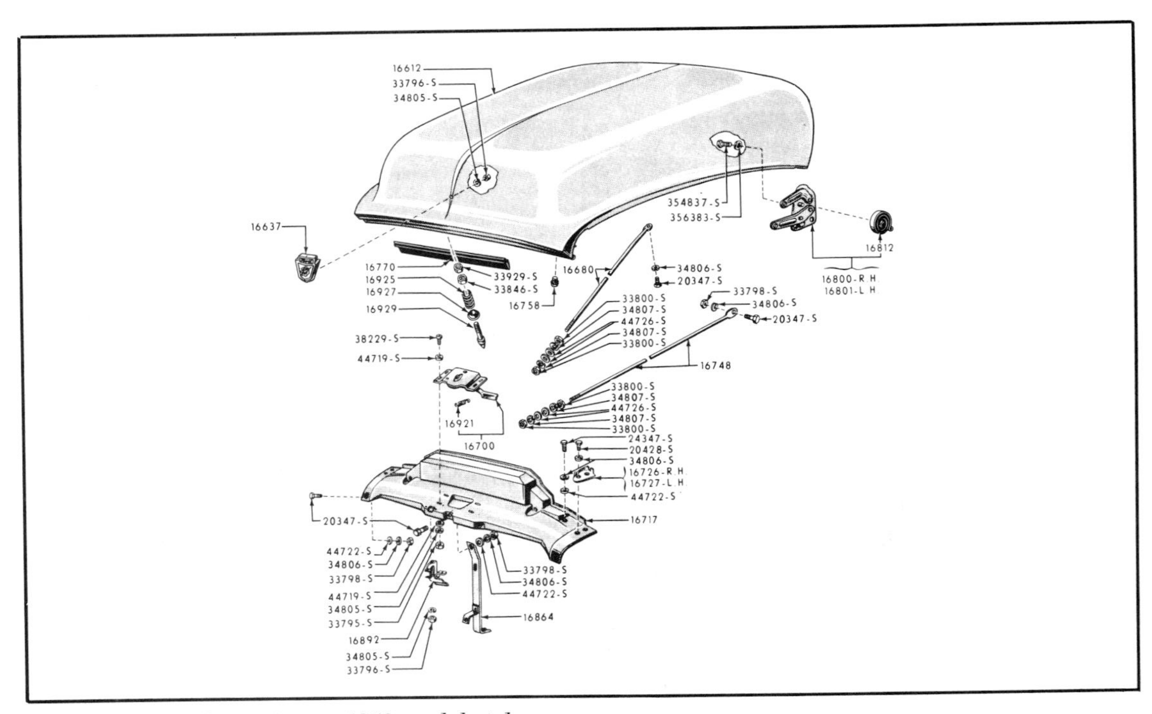

Hood and related parts from a 1956 model pickup.

Chapter 5

Current trends and truck rodding

Of all the models and years represented during this era, the 1953-56 F-100 pickups are by far the most popular. And among them, the 1956 seems to be at the top of the list, especially the Custom Cab Big Window version.

Why is this so? The main reason is its unique styling due to a revamping of the body structure to accommodate the wraparound windshield. For me, this truck best exemplifies the whole fifties mystique. However, no matter which half-ton F-100 you choose, you can rest assured that they are all "cult trucks," each with legions of dedicated fans.

Though the other Ford light-duty commercial vehicles must walk in the shadow of the F-100s, all of them come from good stock—there's not a bad one in the bunch. And when restored, any of these vehicles will stand out in any crowd.

When it comes to restoring Ford trucks of this era there are two schools of thought. On the one hand there are those who will

Classic lines of this 1950 F-1 are shown well by the custom treatment it received: custom wheels and tires, later grille, mirrors, and custom paint and pinstriping.

restore them to 100 percent stock, factory specifications. The other group will also restore them to like-new condition, but in a way to serve the needs of personal tastes rather than following the factory plan. At the moment the latter individuals outnumber the former by a large margin. As a matter of fact, 100 percent factory restorations are few and far between. No matter which restoration you choose—100 percent stock, fully modified or something in between—your vehicle will look just right.

Parts and accessories are, for the most part, easy to come by. Sources can be your local Ford dealer, junkyards and parts houses specializing in these models. In fact, there has been an increase in the number of businesses catering to the truck enthusiast, providing such goodies as fenders, wheels, tires, remanufactured rubber and wood pieces, along with chrome accessories, interior kits, suspension pieces and much, much more.

With all this help, it's possible to build a truck from scratch! All you need is a body and some money. And depending on condition, the amount could be small or large. A good thing to keep in mind the next time you contemplate buying one is to try to get the best possible condition of vehicle so it won't strain your pocketbook.

If you choose to go the factory restoration route you'll need some reference materials to use as guides. The best materials on the subject are original sales and marketing information, body and parts illustrations, and shop manuals. If you choose to restore your

Readily observable features of this black 1950 F-1 customized front end include a full bright orange flame paint job and a custom-chromed tube grille.

vehicle to reflect your own personal tastes, your job may be easier—it all depends on the extent of the modifications you have planned.

No matter which way you choose to go, your main objective should be to produce a sharp-looking truck, so you should concentrate on cleaning up the vehicle to the best of your ability. Detail and paint the underhood area, interior, exterior, bed area and undercarriage. Once that's done you can concentrate on personalizing your truck.

The first thing that you can change is the wheels and tires. A nice set of custom wheels

Note that this 1953 with 1956 hood trim has an opposite-opening hood.

These fine 1953-56 examples were photographed at the 1985 North/South Run at Fresno, California.

The run is sponsored by F-100 Elites and Pickups Ltd of So California.

and tires is a very good starting point. Even such a small change is enough to make a personal statement. If that's not enough for you, you may want to consider installing a dropped front axle. Dropping the front end a few inches will give your vehicle the perfect "street cruiser" stance.

Next on the agenda might be to add a little more brightwork; a little more chrome here and there will add a little more luster to your jewel. In the fifties, Ford kept the glitter to a minimum in its truck lines; after all, these were utility vehicles. So there's plenty of room to add adornment without fear of getting flashy. One of the most popular dress-up items today is a chrome stock grille. (The only Ford truck of this era to come from the factory with a chrome grille was the 1956 Custom Cab.) Just remember when adding chrome, too much of a good thing can spoil the effect, so try not to go overboard.

If you want a truck with the "muscle" look you may want to consider putting a little more punch under the hood, to back up its image. There is a wide range of choices at hand, as long as your engine is a V-8. If you have a six under the hood, your hop-up choices are rather slim, except for a header or two, a cam and a carb. If you want a hotter truck you'll probably be better off with a V-8.

In the V-8 ranks, whether you have a flathead or an overhead valve type, you'll find parts available to put more punch under your pedal. Headers and cams, multiple carbs and so on will usually do the trick. Parts are a little easier to find for the Y-blocks than for their flattie cousins. And if you like to stay "genuine" with Ford Motor Company high-

Tilt nose on this 1955 allows for easy access to all underhood areas.

performance goodies, you are in luck because Ford was involved in big-time auto racing from 1955 to 1957, and it released some parts that can really perk up those Y-blocks. Dual carbs, triple deuces and even a factory supercharger were available. Not only will these engine parts add spark but they'll also get you plenty of "oohs" and "aahs" whenever you pop the hood. These older performance parts can usually be found at more major swap meets; a little looking is all it takes. However, these parts are in demand, so when you do find them, they probably won't be cheap. Don't forget to add a set of finned Thunderbird valve covers—they are always a big hit!

If "genuine" stock isn't your cup of tea, there's plenty of room in those engine compartments to run just about any modern V-8 you choose. If you want to stay in the Ford camp, you can run a small-block—289, 302, 351(C and W), Boss 302, Boss 351—or you can run one of the big-blocks—352, 360, 390, 406, 427, 428, 429 and so forth. If you want to run a General Motors engine or a Chrysler engine, you can do that too. In most cases there are adapters available for any engine you wish. (I've seen a Boss 429 in an early F-1, and I have seen a few blown Ford small-blocks.) All the engines fit under the hood, so nobody has any idea what you are running—voilà, the perfect "sleeper."

With the powertrain taken care of, you can work on your truck's appearance some more, or add a few creature comforts. How about a set of bucket seats, or a six-way adjustable bench? What about air conditioning, tinted glass or a stereo? And don't forget power steering, power disc brakes or a tilt wheel. How about punching a set of louvers in the hood for that cool "fifties" look? And how about getting a neat-fitting tarp to cover your bed, or going all out and opting for a one-piece, tilting front end?

Another item to consider is drivability. Trucks of this period were Spartan in nature; they lacked many of the conveniences we take for granted today. For instance, today's independent front suspensions are quite an improvement over the original straight-bar variety. Many owners opt for the better riding

Personalized license plates are popular, as on this 1955.

Owners can modify their vehicles in many ways. The vanity plate on this 1955 is a good example.

quality of independent front suspensions and they swap for a late-model front frame clip. These subframes are found in late-model, mid-size cars from Ford, General Motors or Chrysler. Thus, for a little extra work and a little extra cash, an owner can get the best of both worlds—the "classic" looks of the old and the modern conveniences and easier driving of the new.

You could also have a nice custom paint job to finish it all off—the crowning touch for a personalized street machine.

A few years ago, a term was coined to describe people who liked to modify trucks. The vehicles were called "truck rods" and the people who liked to "hot rod" them were "truck rodders." Their counterparts—the people who liked to stay within the strict confines of factory stock—were called "truck restorers." Nowdays, the former seems to far outnumber the latter. Why, nobody seems to know for sure, but I suspect the reason may lie in the fact that for a number of years the serious restorers stayed away from commercial vehicles, leaving the market to the "rodders." Because of that you'll see a lot more modified trucks these days; some say the ratio may be ten to one.

Like most auto phenomena of the last forty years, the truck rodding movement had its roots in California, dating from the mid-fifties, when people were just starting to dress up trucks. And when it came to trucks that made good "rodding" material, the first choice was the classic 1953-56 F-100.

Fifties truck rodders commonly dressed up their "Henry Haulers" with a set of spun-aluminum "moon" disc wheel covers, a set of

Phil De La O of New Mexico owns this 1956 modified F-100 with custom wheels and tires, 302 Ford V-8 and custom paint.

This 1985 photo shows custom wheels and tires and smoked glass.

This bright red 1956 F-100 sports a few personalized accessories installed by the owner. They include a later-model Ford passenger car bumper along with the chrome 1956 Custom Cab grille. West Coast mirrors (usually found on larger trucks), custom wheels and tires, and a white tonneau cover have also been added. This truck has a nice white pinstripe, and the overdrive script under the Ford crest indicates it's equipped with the optional overdrive transmission.

"lakes pipes" and a pair of "dummy spots" (spotlights that weren't functional, just for appearance). Some even ventured to have a custom paint job, usually highlighted by flames or a scallop design. If the truck rodder wanted to change powerplants, the most popular choices were the Cadillac engine or Chrysler Hemi engine.

There were some small changes during the sixties for the truck rodding movement. The favored powerplant seemed to be the big-block FE Ford engines; the 390, 406 and 427 engines became pretty popular. There were still people who chose non-Ford engines, but their numbers were diminishing. Truck rodders liked to make changes, but they also liked to stay within the Ford family. Custom flame paint jobs became passé and were replaced by tastefully done pinstripe-highlighted paint jobs.

In the seventies, when oil embargoes became commonplace, the truck rodders turned to the small-block Ford powerplants; engines such as the 289 and 302 went to the top of the popularity list. Those engines provided enough power in a small package, and they gave better fuel economy than their bigger-cubed brothers. Good-quality fiberglass pieces became available, giving the truck rodder a choice between sheet metal and lighter-weight glass components. The auto buff magazines rediscovered custom trucks and featured more of them.

The dawning of the eighties brought more interest in truck rodding, as even more people fell under the customizing spell.

Customized 1956 F-100 with tinted glass, chrome running board, tonneau cover, wire wheels and chrome Custom Cab trim.

The truck rodder who came up with this slogan for a 1956 is to be congratulated.

This 1956 has been personalized with pinstriping around its badge.

This work truck, nicknamed Crazy Coyote, is a 1956 vintage F-100. Power is supplied by a highly modified 429 ci Ford engine. It's popular on the tractor-pulling contest circuit.

Ford truck crest running board step plate, a popular accessory for custom truck owners.

This 1956 F-100 has been customized by punching a couple of louvers in the hood, adding some tasteful pinstriping and painting the stylized Ford script onto the cowl vent mesh screen.

Trucking enthusiasts even had their own magazine, *Truckin'*, which featured the trucking field from coast to coast. Trucking meets became more popular too, being held in towns across the United States (no longer limited to the state of California). The last one I attended had 200 trucks on hand. And that meet was only a regional affair; national events can attract even more participants.

When it comes to good looks, these Ford trucks have it all—stock or hot, mild or wild. If you choose to restore your truck to 100 percent stock specifications, you won't be disappointed. And if you choose to personalize it, maybe making it a truck rod, remember—the sky's the limit!

The "bra" used on this 1956 helps keep rock and bug damage to a minimum on the tilt nose.

This modified 1956 Custom Cab F-100 has the Big Window feature. Photo taken at the 1985 North/South Run.

Chrome bed header panel certainly makes the oak bed panel strips look longer. This is a modified 1956 Big Window Custom Cab F-100. Photo taken at the 1985 North/South Run.

Chapter 6

The conversion factor

In the previous chapters I discussed how Ford tried to cover all the bases in the light-duty commercial field. Other manufacturers also tried hard, but some buyers in the market had special needs that weren't covered by the normal factory cataloged offerings. This is where the specialty market and its venders came into play. These firms offered conversions in the body, chassis and powertrain. Their conversions weren't meant to replace the usual factory offerings, but to complement them. These outside venders helped to fill the little niches that weren't cost effective for the big manufacturers.

Quite a few conversions were done on Ford trucks during this time. The most notable was modifying Ford trucks from a two-wheel-drive layout to that of a four-wheel, or all-wheel, layout. (Prior to 1959 Ford didn't offer a factory four-wheel-drive unit.) The job was done one of two ways: Either the buyer made arrangements with the converter or the Ford salesperson specified that the truck be shipped to the vender and, when completed, shipped on to the dealership for delivery to the customer.

The two most famous converters doing these types of modification were the American Coleman Company and the better-known (and discussed here) Marmon-Herrington Company.

The Marmon-Herrington group offered two conversion ranges, one for the light-duty half-tons, and the other for the three-quarter-ton and three-quarter-ton heavy-duty models. Both versions came standard with a four-speed transmission, beefed-up springs and shocks, special hardened axle shafts and beefed-up carriers. They differed only in the type of transfer case that was used. The light-duty version used a single-range case while the heavy-duty variety used a dual-range case. When the dual-range case was combined with the standard four-speed transmission, the heavy-duties had a total of eight forward speeds—just the ticket for off-road use, where one could never be sure what type of driving situations might be encountered.

All of these conversions sat quite a bit higher than their stock counterparts—though not as high as some of today's conversions, in which a four wheeler takes on the appearance of a giant, and the cab is placed up in nose-bleed territory. Back then, "high" meant twelve inches or so higher than stock. The height was gained because the springs carried extra leaves between the frame and the axle. The main reason for lifting the body and frame farther off the ground was to gain a safe clearance for the axle housing and transfer case. A bonus of all this beefing was that these trucks gained a heavier gross vehicle weight rating, meaning they could carry heavier loads. These were rough, tough trucks with a reputation of being as strong as tanks.

The Marmon-Herrington conversion could be had on any Ford light-duty model with any body style. Marmon-Herrington also offered one body style that wasn't carried in the regular Ford lineup. This unique model was called the Ranger and it featured a seven-passenger interior housed in a window-type van body. The body itself was a modification of Ford's panel van (no side windows) model, and it was similar in appearance to Chevrolet's Suburban. The Ranger was great for hauling work crews out to remote job sites, for example.

In the mid-fifties, all-wheel-drive and four-wheel-drive units were popular with utility companies, construction companies and oil- and gas-drilling outfits. Exact production figures for these rare and unusual trucks don't exist today but you can be sure that even when new these converted trucks were low in numbers. The four-wheel-drive market back then was a small and specialized field, not like the booming four-wheel-drive recreational market of today. Those trucks were meant for hard work, and plenty of it—nobody thought they could be used for fun. Most of them led rough lives and few remain today, so finding one can be a long and arduous procedure. Still, if you like challenges, this type of treasure hunt may just be up your alley; there are still some diamonds in the rough out there. Do your searching around drilling areas and other remote sites. Who knows, your efforts may be rewarded.

This 1953 4x4 conversion is a more modern adaptation. This owner simply mounted an old body on a newer 4x4 chassis—a far easier job than the original Marmon-Herrington units, which had to be converted into an "all-wheel-drive" unit. Photo taken in 1985 at the North/South Run at Fresno, California.

Chapter 7

The Canadian connection

Starting in 1946 and continuing through 1956, truck buyers in Canada had a choice of two nameplates (but just one engine, V-8) on Ford commercial vehicles built in Canada. One was the Ford line which was sold through Canadian Ford dealers. These vehicles, except for a few items, were exactly the same as their US counterparts. Almost everything on them was shared, and one could only tell them apart through serial number designations and other codes. The other offering in Canada, the Mercury, looked identical to the Ford line from a distance, but it had enough trim differences to set it apart. It was sold by Mercury dealers throughout Canada.

Though the two lines wore different trims and each was sold through different dealer networks, they were built at the same time, at the same assembly plant in Windsor, Ontario. They shared the same bodies, chassis, engines, driveline components and almost everything else, so building the two trucks on the same line posed few problems.

Canadian Ford trucks carried the same model designations (F-1, F-2 and F-3) as US versions, while the Mercury line of light commercial vehicles carried different designations: M-47 for the half-ton version and M-68 for the three-quarter-ton version. When the nomenclature changed on the Ford truck lines in 1953 to F-100, F-250 and F-350, the Mercury line was changed to M-100, M-250 and M-350.

In 1948, Mercury trucks were touted as the Smartest Truck Line Ever Built. If "smart" meant sharp, good looks, that claim may have been true. Mercury trucks were dressed up with all sorts of bright trim items not found on the more common Ford versions. That brightwork helped them to stand out from the competition and made it easier to sell them at a higher price. Mercury dealers in Canada wanted a good-looking truck to offer their customers, and the Mercury line provided it.

Ford of Canada also exported trucks to foreign markets like Australia, New Zealand, South Africa and other British Commonwealth countries (except for Great Britain). A few Mercury trucks might also have immigrated to the United States.

If you are looking for a truly unique Ford truck from this period, give serious consideration to finding a Mercury version. You don't see many of these trucks today because Mercury truck production was much lower than Ford truck production in the US or Canada. A 1948-56 Mercury truck is an attention-getter today.

The chrome trim on the fenders and body sides of this 1948 prototype did not appear on production US vehicles. However, the brightwork did appear on Canadian Mercury trucks.

F-1

Chapter 8

Toys and other collectibles

From the late forties through the mid-fifties, when Ford Motor Company was building these trucks, the toy manufacturers were busy producing small replicas that rivaled the bigger versions in popularity.

There was hardly a boy back then (me included) who didn't want a toy Ford truck to play with. With such a high demand, the toy manufacturers were selling just as many little ones as Ford was building big ones. Companies like Tonka, Buddy L, Tootsietoy and Revell produced Ford-related miniatures. There were others, but these produced the most. Their creations were so detailed that collectors today are scouring the countryside for them.

Of all the companies, Tonka was the biggest. From pickup trucks to trailer truck rigs, Tonka had something to offer everyone. Its trucks were made out of the same gauge of steel as their bigger counterparts, so they were more than up to the rigors of rough playing over the years. These trucks were the perfect size for sandbox play, about twelve inches long (the pickups) and about eight inches tall.

Tootsietoys were also available as smaller-scale (1/32 and 1/43) diecast Ford pickup miniatures. Tootsietoys could also be used in the sandbox, but they were better suited to table-top playing. Though the Tootsietoys looked like the real Fords, I feel that the Tonka trucks had better detail.

A couple of promotional toys were produced by private companies and distributed through Ford parts departments. I have never seen any of these, though I suspect that Banthrico and AMT might have been responsible for their manufacture, since both of those companies were producing Ford promotionals at that time. These models are highly sought after by promotional collectors as well as trucking enthusiasts. They are harder to find than the Tonkas and Tootsietoys, so their prices will be higher. Though other promotional models may have been available at that time for Ford trucks, the two best known are a 1951 Ford panel truck and a 1953 F-100 pickup.

Besides the promotional models, model kits were available to test the skills of budding young truck enthusiasts. Revell was one of the first model makers to offer a Ford truck kit. I recently found a 1/43 scale kit of the 1956 Ford pickup. This kit was unbuilt and still in the original box. I felt very lucky to have found one in such good condition (the last time I saw one of these was almost thirty years ago, on display in a drug store window). The original box price was around a dollar, but I assure you it cost that and more to convince its previous owner to part with it.

In the early sixties, Revell released a larger-scale 1956 Ford pickup kit. This 1/25 scale model featured an opening hood and doors, and highly detailed chassis, engine and interior parts. At the same time, AMT released a 1/25 scale 1953 Ford pickup kit. Though not as detailed as the Revell version, it is nice. Like the Revell kit it features an opening hood with one of the best-looking flathead engines this side of a James Dean Mercury. These two kits have been rereleased a number of times over the last twenty years, so you don't have to pay high collector prices for them. MPC and Monogram now have 1953-56 Ford pickup models, so the toy buyers and model builders have a variety of choices.

In the smaller scale, Matchbox has some mid-fifties Ford pickups available. At last count there were three versions available: a regular pickup with motorcycles in the bed, a camper-shell pickup and an off-road racing version. As far as I know, nobody is making models of the 1948-52 F-1, F-2 or F-3 Ford pickups. Monogram released a street rod version of a 1955 Ford panel truck a couple of years ago. You may still be able to find one in a toy store.

A few weeks ago I met Preston Ledbetter of California. Preston is well known in Ford truck collector circles because he has served collectors' parts needs since 1956. Besides selling parts, Preston collects Ford trucks of fifties vintage. He also collects Ford truck toys, a fact not known by many people. At last count, Preston's Ford truck toy collection numbered 3,000 units, most of them Tonkas. To have that many toys requires dedication, and as far as I know his is the largest Ford toy collection in the world.

In addition to toys, quite a few other Ford items are collectible. These items run the gamut from printed pieces and photographs to lapel pins, and much more.

These belong to Paul McLaughlin of New Mexico.

Though pieces like catalogs, sales materials and magazine advertisements are harder to find than their auto-related counterparts, Ford did offer them during this period. In practically every model year the company offered complete-line catalogs as well as catalogs and folders that dealt specifically with a certain model. There were separate examples for the F-1, F-2, F-3, F-100, F-250 and F-350. These contained illustrations of the exteriors and interiors, and they sometimes carried photographs of available optional equipment. And, since these were commercial vehicles, they often carried detailed specification sheets, which included just about all the information that one might ever ask. Look for these items at swap meets or through literature dealers. Since commercial vehicles haven't caught on with serious collectors, prices should be reasonable. Other items of this nature to look for are 16 mm training films, postcards and salesmen's data books.

If your truck needs some mechanical work, try to pick up a shop manual for it. These manuals have so much to offer that you shouldn't be without one. Originals are still available at swap meets, or you can get a new, reprinted, clean version. You might also want to pick up a copy of the body parts catalog for

Some old and new Ford truck model kits and toys from my collection.

your Ford truck. These illustrated books show exploded drawings of parts and how they interface with other parts. They also list part numbers, which can help if you need to order or look for parts. Because of those exploded-view drawings, these are a must for your technical library and Ford truck literature collection.

You might want to start canvassing the local used magazine dealers for copies of magazines of this period. Sometimes Ford used photographs and sometimes illustrations in its advertising campaigns. Look in magazines like *Life*, *Look*, *Time* and *Newsweek* and in farming and trucking magazines. Truck advertisements are not as easy to find as car ads because Ford didn't advertise its truck line as much as its car line—but with a little effort you should be able to find the piece you want. When you get your ads, frame them; they make nice wall hangings.

Other period paperwork to collect are the owners manuals because they perform a two-fold service: They provide information on the proper use of your vehicle, and they look neat, at shows, displayed in the truck's interior.

You might start a photograph collection of 8x10, black-and-white factory glossies, though finding photographs from this period may be harder than you think (I am speaking from first-hand knowledge). The best place to find photos is at the bigger swap meets held around the country. You might also want to photograph your own truck and those of your buddies.

You could also start a jewelry collection. Original period pieces came only as tie bars and an occasional lapel pin. However, there are quite a few new pieces that might appeal to you. If you like hat pins or lapel pins, you are in luck; dealers are carrying pins that depict the miniature Ford truck crest, miniature side-model identification pieces (F-100, for example) as well as miniature Ford pickup

Monogram Models put out this 1955 Ford panel truck.

trucks. You can also find tee-shirts, belt buckles, hats and so on to display your pride in Ford trucks of this era. Most of these items are geared to the 1953-56 owner, but perhaps items of this nature will also become available for the earlier years.

Of course, this short chapter can't begin to cover everything that is available to collectors. But then, the search is half the fun. Who knows? You may find your collection of toys and other memorabilia growing as rapidly as your collection of the big Ford trucks!

This 1955 Tonka Toys truck is from the collection of George Hinds.

Accessories and optional equipment

Though its light commercial vehicles of this era carried quite a bit of standard equipment, Ford felt the market might want extra equipment, so an extensive option list was made available. When this era began in 1948, there were just a few items to choose from—which was all buyers demanded. In the fifties, buyers started demanding and getting even more optional equipment.

The following is a list of what the factory offered when these vehicles were new, just in case you want to upgrade your stock or modified vehicle with period accessories.

1948-50
Spotlight
Rear bumper
White sidewall tires
Wheel beauty trim rings
Locking gas cap
Radio
Grille guard
Heavy-duty fan
Right-hand windshield wiper
Heavy-duty 3-speed manual transmission (49)
4-speed manual transmission (standard on F-2, F-3)
Heater and defroster
Heavy-duty radiator
Right-hand rear taillight
Right-hand sun visor
Rear axle ratios (4.09, 4.27)
Seat covers
Chrome grille bars
Oil filter
Safety reflector kit
Windshield washer
Fire extinguisher
Engine compartment lamp
Turn indicator lamps
Utility lamp
Electric shaver

1951
Oil filter
Rear axle ratios (4.09, 4.27)
Heater and defroster
Right-hand rear taillight
11-inch clutch disc
Deluxe cab
Extra front seat for panel truck
4-speed transmission (standard on F-2 and F-3)
Electric windshield wipers
Rear bumper
Heavy-duty fan
Heavy-duty radiator
Heavy-duty 3-speed manual transmission

1952
Right-hand visor
Deluxe Five Star cab
Locking gas cap
Seat covers
Rear bumper
Radio
Grille guard
Fire extinguisher
Oil filter
Windshield washer
Heater and defroster
4-speed manual transmission (standard on F-2 and F-3)
Engine compartment lamp
11-inch clutch
Heavy-duty battery
Turn signal lamps

Heavy-duty radiator
Heavy-duty 3-speed manual transmission
Extra seat for panel truck

1953
Tinted glass
Locking gas cap
Hand throttle
Heavy-duty generator
Flare set
Rear axle ratios
Ford-O-Matic transmission
Deluxe Five Star cab
Grille guard
3-speed with overdrive manual transmission
Rear bumper
4-speed manual transmission
Heavy-duty fan
Oil filter
Electric windshield wipers
Heater and defroster
Deluxe radio
Seat covers
Windshield washer
Outside rearview mirrors
Tow hooks
Turn signals
Extra seat for panel truck

1954
Rear axle ratios (4.09, 4.27)
Vacuum-boosted power brakes
Rear bumper
Deluxe cab
Spare wheel side carrier mount
Ford-O-Matic transmission
Heater and defroster
Oil filter
Heavy-duty radiator
Right-hand taillight
Outside rearview mirrors
Shock absorbers
Deluxe radio
Wheels and tires
Cigar lighter
11-inch heavy-duty clutch
Tow hooks
Turn signal lamps
Fire extinguisher
Chrome hood crest molding
3-speed with overdrive transmission
Electric windshield wipers

1955
120 amp hour battery
Oil filter
Vacuum-boosted power brakes
Side-mount spare tire carrier
Custom cab
Turn signal lamps
Engine compartment lamps
Heater and defroster
Locking gas cap
11 inch heavy-duty clutch
Tinted glass
Outside rearview mirrors
Windshield washer
Extra seat for panel truck
Power steering
Electric windshield wipers
Oil filter
Grille guard
Road lamps
Heavy-duty springs
Seat covers
Stop lamp
Right-hand rear taillight
Tow hooks
Visor
3-speed overdrive transmission

1956
Same as 1955 with safety items (seat belts, deep-dish steering wheel) and chrome grille

Ford-Designed Accessories for '54

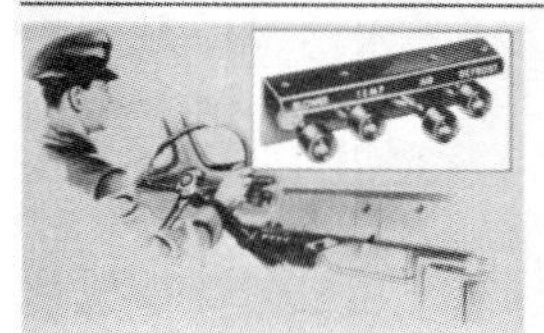

MagicAire Heating, Defrosting and Ventilating system. Year 'round comfort

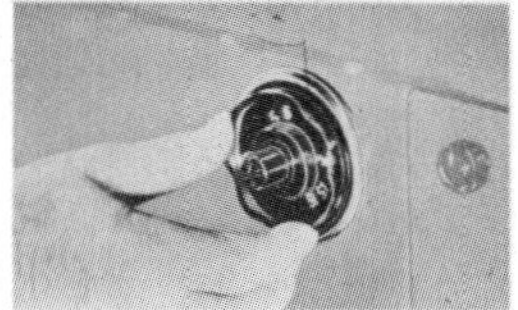

Truck radio — Five tubes plus rectifier Overhead speaker. Notched dial contro

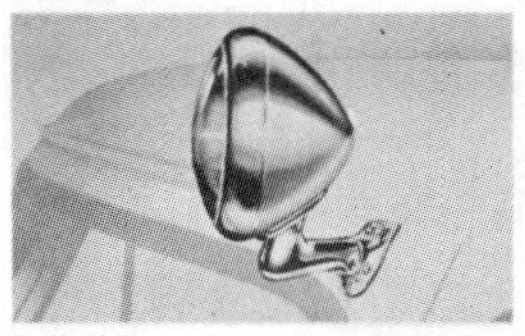

Sealed Beam Spotlight with bracket. Can be aimed in almost any direction

See-Clear Windshield Washer removes road grime for relaxed, safer driving

Radiator Grille Guards. Heavy-duty type

Front Tow Hooks for emergency towing or pulling

Built for your Ford Truck
At your Ford Dealer's now

Many other Ford Truck special parts and accessories available, including:

Sealed Beam Road Lamps for maximum glare-free light . . . **Stop Lamp,** 8-in. dia., red lens with universal bracket . . . **Fire Extinguisher,** 1½-qt. . . . **Reflector Flare Set,** complete kit, three flares, flags, flagstaffs . . . **Extension Arm Mirror,** six-inch adjustment . . . **Mirror Arm Braces** . . . **Heavy-Duty Generator,** 32-amp. low cut-in, 60-amp. . . . **Heavy Duty Batteries,** 100-amp. hr., 120-amp. hr., 136-amp. hr., 155-amp. hr. . . . **Directional Turn Signals,** flasher type. Self-canceling.

All priced right! Get what you need to make your job safer, pleasanter, easier. See your Ford Dealer!

Ford-designed accessories for 1954. Clues, *January-February 1954*

NOW! Power Braking for Pickups!

Only on Ford! Now—you can have Power Braking on your new '54 Pickup, or Panel, or any Ford ½-ton model at extra cost. Easier, *safer* control . . . does up to one-fourth the work of stopping for you!

Now—*Fordomatic Drive* is available at extra cost on all Ford light-duty models for '54. Fully automatic —no manual shifting—no clutch work!

Now — gas-saving, low-friction, high-compression, overhead valve, deep-block engines in *all* new Ford Truck models! V-8 and Six.

NEW FORD FIRST!

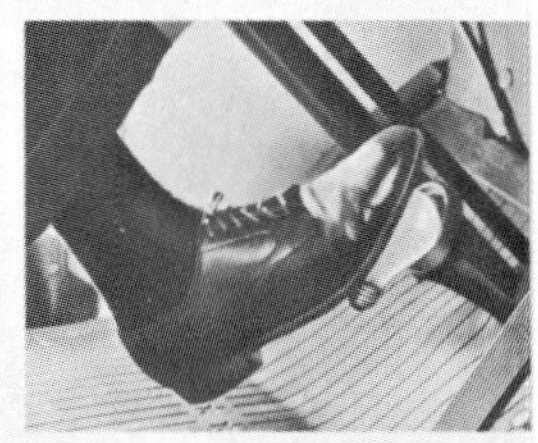

Pressure needed to stop truck with New Ford Power Brakes is not enough to break this light bulb!

SEE THEM TODAY!

FORD Triple Economy **TRUCKS**

Clues, *March 1954*

The 1955 F-100 carries the optional side-mounted spare tire. This option required a special bracket and a modified left rear fender.

Engines and transmissions

Engine
Year: 1948-51
Type: Rouge 226
Ford code: 7HT
Cylinders: 6
Bore: 3.3 in.
Stroke: 4.4 in.
Displacement: 226 ci
Compression ratio: 6.8:1
Carburetor: single downdraft
Gross horsepower: 95 bhp at 3300 rpm
Net horsepower (with accessories): 87 bhp at 3100 rpm
Gross torque: 180 lb-ft at 1200 rpm
Net torque: 178 lb-ft at 1200 rpm
Design: L-head
Note: Ford called these engines Cost Clippers.

Year: 1948-51
Type: Rouge 239 V-8
Ford code: 8RT
Cylinders: 8
Bore: 3-3/16 in.
Stroke: 3¾ in.
Displacement: 239 ci
Compression ratio: 6.8:1
Carburetor: downdraft
Gross horsepower: 100 at 3800 rpm
Net horsepower (with accessories): 90 at 3500 rpm
Gross torque: 180 lb-ft at 2000 rpm
Net torque: 178 lb-ft at 1600 rpm
Design: flathead

Year: 1952-53
Type: Cost Clipper
Ford code: D
Cylinders: 6
Bore: 3.56 in.
Stroke: 3.6 in.
Displacement: 215 ci
Compression ratio: 7.0:1
Carburetor: single downdraft venturi
Gross horsepower: 101 at 3500 rpm
Gross torque: 185 lb-ft reached between 1300-1700 rpm
Design: ohv
Note: First use of overhead valve design engine in a Ford light-duty commercial vehicle.

Year: 1952-53
Type: Rouge 239 V-8
Ford code: R
Cylinders: 8
Bore: 3.1875 in.
Stroke: 3.75 in.
Displacement: 239 ci
Compression ratio: 6.8:1
Carburetor: dual downdraft
Gross horsepower: 106 at 3500 rpm (due mostly to a higher-lift camshaft)
Gross torque: 194 lb-ft between 1900 and 2100 rpm
Design: flathead
Note: 1953 was last year for flathead use in US Ford vehicles.

Year: 1954-55
Type: Cost Clipper
Ford code: D
Cylinders: 6
Bore: 3.62 in.
Stroke: 3.60 in.
Displacement: 223 ci
Compression ratio: 7.5:1 (1955), 7.2:1 (1954)
Carburetor: single venturi downdraft

Gross horsepower: 115 at 3800 rpm (1954), 118 (1955)
Net horsepower: 109 at 3600 rpm
Gross torque: 195 lb-ft at 1200-2400 rpm (1955), 193 (1954)
Net torque: 189 lb-ft at 1000-2300 rpm
Design: ohv
Note: Built in Cleveland.

Year: 1954-55
Type: Power King V-8 Y-Block
Ford code: V
Cylinders: 8
Bore: 3.50 in.
Stroke: 3.10 in.
Displacement: 239 ci (same as flathead)
Compression ratio: 7.5:1 (1955), 7.2:1 (1954)
Carburetor: dual venturi downdraft
Gross horsepower: 130-132 bhp at 4200 rpm
Net horsepower: 113.5 bhp at 3600 rpm
Gross torque: 215 lb-ft at 1800-2200 rpm, 214 (1954)
Net torque: 209 lb-ft at 1500-2000 rpm
Design: overhead valve
Note: Engines built at Rouge plant in 1954, at Cleveland in 1955

Year: 1956
Type: Cost Cutter
Ford code: D
Cylinders: 6
Bore: 3.62 in.
Stroke: 3.60 in.
Displacement: 223 ci
Compression ratio: 7.8:1
Carburetor: single venturi downdraft
Gross horsepower: 133 bhp at 4000 rpm
Gross torque: 202 lb-ft at 1600-2600 rpm
Design: overhead valve
Note: Engines built in Cleveland.

Year: 1956
Type: Power King V-8
Ford code: V
Cylinders: 8
Bore: 3.62 in.
Stroke: 3.30 in.
Displacement: 272 ci
Compression ratio: 7.8:1
Carburetor: dual venturi downdraft
Gross horsepower: 167 bhp at 4400 rpm
Gross torque: 260 lb-ft at 2100-2600 rpm
Design: overhead valve
Note: These were the engines that Ford listed for light-duty commercial vehicles during this time period. Ford had larger engines available for its bigger trucks.

Transmission

Year: 1948-52

A. 1. 3-speed manual with synchronizers (floor shift 1948-50, column shift from 9/50) standard on F-1
   2. 3-speed heavy-duty manual (floor shift) optional on F-1, F-2 and F-3. Warner T87D transmission (starting in 1949).
   3. 4-speed manual standard on F-2 and F-3

B. 1. 1-piece driveshaft on F-1
   2. 2-piece driveshaft on F-2 and F-3

C. 1. 10-inch clutch disc standard on F-1
   2. 11-inch clutch standard on F-2 and F-3, optional on F-1

D. Differential gearing
   1. F-1 models, 3.73 standard 1948-50, 3.92 standard 1951-52, 4.27 optional (all years)
   2. F-2 and F-3, 4.86 standard (all years)

Year: 1953-56

A. 1. 3-speed manual (column shift) standard F-100
   2. 3-speed manual (column shift) heavy-duty standard on F-250 and F-350, optional on F-100
   3. 3-speed manual (column shift) medium-duty standard on F-250 (1956), optional on F-100 (1956)
   4. Ford-O-Matic automatic (column shift) optional on all models—F-100 (1953-56), F-250 and F-350 (1954-56)
   5. 4-speed manual (floor shift) optional on all models—F-100, F-250, F-350
   6. 3-speed manual with overdrive (column shift) optional on F-100

B. 1. 1-piece driveshaft on F-100 models (except 2-piece on long-wheelbase 118″ introduced in 1956)
   2. 2-piece driveshaft on F-250 and F-350 models

C. 1. 10-inch clutch standard on F-100 models (1953-56 6-cylinder, 1953-55 V-8), standard on F-250 models (1953-55)
   2. 10½ inch clutch standard on F-100 (V-8) models (1956), standard on F-250 models (1956)
   3. 11-inch clutch standard on F-350 models (1953-56), optional on F-100 and F-250 models (all years)

D. Axle Ratings
   3.92 F-100 standard
   4.09 F-100 optional
   4.27 F-100 optional (1953-55)
   3.73 F-100 optional (1956)
   4.86 F-250 standard, F-350 standard (1956 only)
   4.56 F-250 optional (1956)
   5.14 F-350 standard (1953-55), optional (1956)
   5.83 F-350 optional (1953-56)

Note: The F-250s and F-350s were considered trucks that would see harder use, so their components were beefed up considerably over their F-100 counterparts.

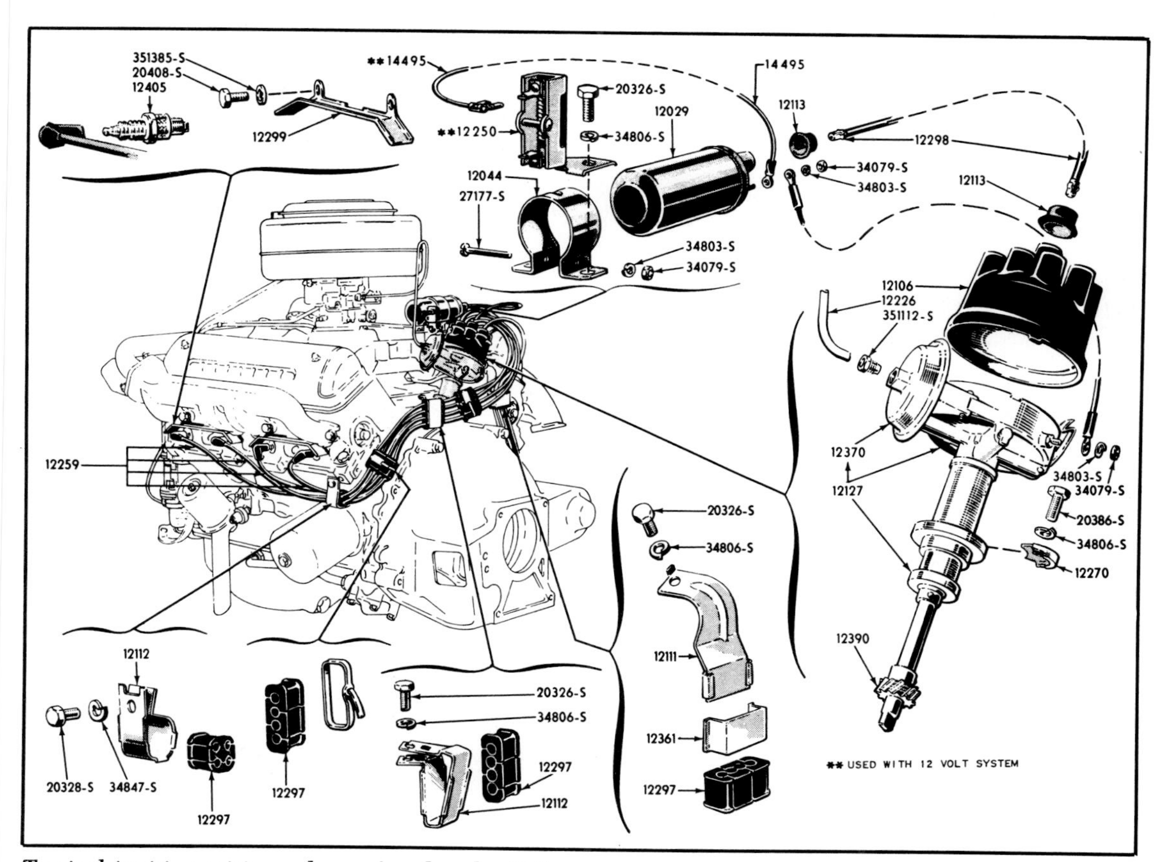

Typical ignition wiring scheme for the ohv V-8 engine.

THE WORLD FAMOUS

FORD 106 H.P. TRUCK V-8

This is the truck engine by which others are judged for economy, performance, and durability.

And Ford has more experience in building V-8 engines than any manufacturer in the world . . .

...MORE THAN 12 MILLION FORD V8'S BUILT SINCE 1932... FOUR OUT OF EVERY FIVE V8'S ON THE ROAD TODAY ARE FORD V8'S

Ford pioneered the V-8 engine design now found in the most expensive cars. Today, the Ford Truck V-8 shows the result of constant improvement to give you the best possible performance with economy.

ALL FORD ENGINES ARE DESIGNED TO OPERATE EFFICIENTLY ON REGULAR GASOLINE—

THE WORLD FAMOUS FORD 106 H.P. V-8 OFFERS...

FULL PRESSURE LUBRICATION

FREE-TURN VALVES   AUTOTHERMIC PISTONS

POWER PILOT ECONOMY

PLUS

ALL THE OTHER OUTSTANDING FORD V-8 FEATURES WHICH HAVE ESTABLISHED THIS ENGINE'S WORLDWIDE REPUTATION FOR SMOOTH, QUIET OPERATION

"The World Famous" flathead Ford V-8 . . . nothing about toughness here, only smoothness and quietness.

302 Ford V-8 with Cobra dress-up kit, headers and power steering (all taken from a later-model Mustang).

454 Chevy with custom carburetion system. Lots of chrome, braided hoses and louvers.

Unrestored 1950 flathead engine compartment. Note oil filter, "oil bath" air cleaner, oil filler pipe, generator mounting.

Details of a 1950 flathead engine compartment (V-8). Note carburetor, oil breather pipe and battery location.

Note wiring on firewall, voltage regulator and battery on this 1950 engine compartment.

Horn relay and headlight wiring ahead of radiator on a 1950.

NEW FOR '52...

THE MOST EFFICIENT SIX-CYLINDER TRUCK ENGINE EVER BUILT

THE FORD 101 H.P. COST CLIPPER VALVE IN HEAD SIX

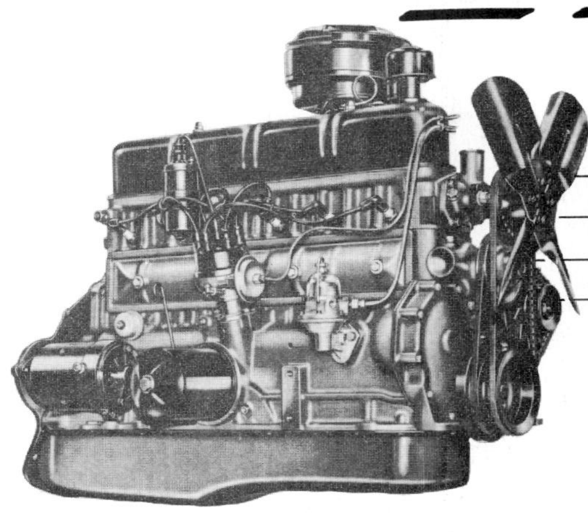

DISPLACEMENT	215 cubic inches
COMPRESSION RATIO	7 to 1
MAX. HORSEPOWER	101 at 3500 r.p.m.
MAX. TORQUE	185 lbs.-ft. at 1300-1700 r.p.m.

THIS NEW FORD-DESIGNED, FORD-PRODUCED VALVE-IN-HEAD SIX IS THE MOST MODERN, EFFICIENT FORD TRUCK ENGINE EVER BUILT.

HIGH COMPRESSION-LOW FRICTION DESIGN

PRODUCES MORE HORSEPOWER PER CUBIC INCH DISPLACEMENT, GIVING YOU MORE ECONOMY... IN FACT, *UP TO 14% BETTER* GAS ECONOMY!

ALL FORD ENGINES ARE DESIGNED TO OPERATE EFFICIENTLY ON REGULAR GASOLINE

Taken from 1952 salesman's guide. Note the words "valve-in-head"; 1952 was the first year an overhead valve arrangement was used in any Ford truck engine.

The *low-price leader* of a great economy line gives you a choice of V-8 or 6-cylinder power!

Only Ford gives you a choice between 6-cylinder and V-8 power—engines truck-designed, truck-engineered and built for trucks by truck builders!

Compare the superior features of the Ford Truck engines! Top compression rings chrome-plated for longest possible service life while conserving oil! New Free-Turn valves for self-cleaning, better seating. Series-Flow cooling for more efficient performance! Improved, high lift camshaft increases valve openings to give greater power and more efficiency. New, lightweight autothermic aluminum alloy pistons for closer dimension-control resulting in quieter operation, more power and lower maintenance costs. New Waterproof ignition designed to assure quick starts under all weather conditions. Replaceable thin shell, steel-backed main and connecting rod bearings.

No matter which engine you choose, you benefit from Ford's Step-Ahead power engineering!

THE FORD 95-HORSEPOWER TRUCK SIX

95 H.P. 180 LBS.-FT. TORQUE

THIS IS TO CERTIFY THAT THE INFORMATION SHOWN ON THIS CURVE SHEET IS CORRECT TO THE BEST OF MY KNOWLEDGE

SIGNED Dale Roeder

EXECUTIVE ENGINEER, COMMERCIAL VEHICLES ENGINEERING, FORD MOTOR COMPANY.

SPECIFICATIONS

- **Type**—6-cylinder "L" head
- **Bore**—3.300 in.
- **Stroke**—4.400 in.
- **Displacement**—226 cu. in.
- **Brake H.P.**—95 at 3,300 r.p.m.
- **Torque**—180 lbs.-ft. at 1,200 r.p.m.
- **Compression Ratio**—6.8 to 1
- **Main Bearings**—Four, 2⅞ in. dia.
  - **Total Area**—43.385 sq. in.
- **Con. Rod Bearings**—2.298 in. dia.
  - **Total Area**—51.980 sq. in.
- **Piston Pins**—Tubular, full-floating
- **Carburetor**—Single downdraft
- **Water Pump**—Centrifugal, packless type
- **Fan**—4-blade, 17 in. dia.
- **Lubrication**—Full pressure
- **Crankcase Capacity with opt. oil filter**—6 qts. (dry), 5 qts. (refill). Clean-out plate in oil pan
- **Oil Bath Air Cleaner**—1 qt. cap., standard equip.

THE FORD 100-HORSEPOWER TRUCK V-8

100 H.P. 180 LBS.-FT. TORQUE

THIS IS TO CERTIFY THAT THE INFORMATION SHOWN ON THIS CURVE SHEET IS CORRECT TO THE BEST OF MY KNOWLEDGE

SIGNED Dale Roeder

EXECUTIVE ENGINEER, COMMERCIAL VEHICLES ENGINEERING, FORD MOTOR COMPANY.

SPECIFICATIONS

- **Type**—V-8 90° "L" head
- **Bore**—3.1875 in.
- **Stroke**—3.75 in.
- **Displacement**—239 cu. in.
- **Brake H.P.**—100 at 3,800 r.p.m.
- **Torque**—180 lbs.-ft. at 2,000 r.p.m.
- **Compression Ratio**—6.8 to 1
- **Main Bearings**—Three, 2.5 in. dia.
  - **Total Area**—38.955 sq. in.
- **Con. Rod Bearings**—(8) 2.1385 in. dia.
  - **Total Area**—41.116 sq. in.
- **Piston Pins**—Tubular, full-floating
- **Carburetor**—Dual downdraft
- **Water Pumps**—Two centrifugal, ball bearing, pre-lubricated
- **Fan**—4-blade, 18½ in. dia.
- **Lubrication**—Full pressure
- **Crankcase Capacity with opt. oil filter**—6 qts. (dry), 5 qts. (refill). Clean-out plate in oil pan
- **Oil Bath Air Cleaner**—1 qt. cap., standard equip.

Flathead six versus flathead V-8. Not much in it for power or torque, although the six peaks for both of these at lower rpm. The date was 1951.

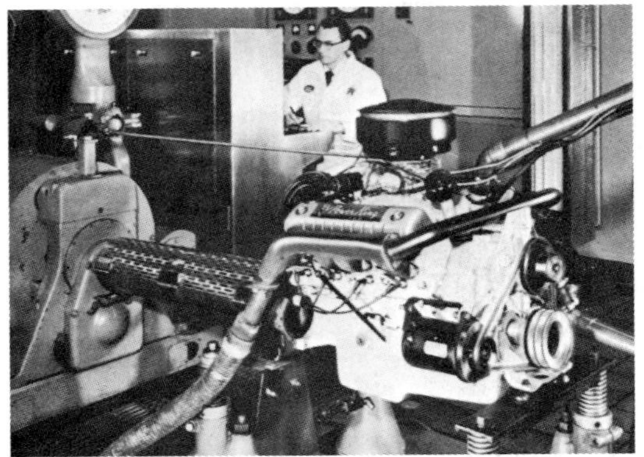

One of the truck industry's most rugged engine endurance tests.

Brutal destruction test proves Ford engine stamina

ABOVE, you see a new Ford short-stroke V-8 truck engine, its exhaust manifold fiery red, nearing the final hour of its piston destruction test on the dynamometer stand at Dearborn. The engine is run wide open, with excessive spark advance and is required to endure that punishment for more than 100 hours. Normally the industry considers 35 hours tops for this kind of punishment. Other ordeals include: the 100-hour endurance run, the 100-hour oil-consumption test and the 150-hour performance test. Let your Ford Dealer show you a Ford Truck short-stroke engine that's built to last longer!

FORD TRIPLE ECONOMY TRUCKS

NEW MONEY MAKERS FOR '55

The big news from Ford in 1955 concerned its new "short-stroke" engines. Ford promoted this aspect of engine design, saying it produced more power with less strain.

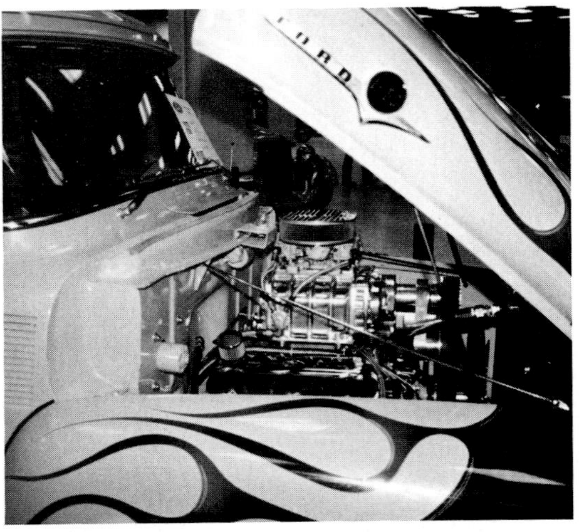

A closer view of Gare Perry's blown Ford 302 V-8, which sits on a Chevelle front frame clip and suspension in his custom 1956 panel.

This 1956 features custom firewall work, 289 engine from a Mustang, headers and lots of chrome.

YOUR CHOICE OF 2 GREAT FORD BONUS BUILT TRUCK ENGINES

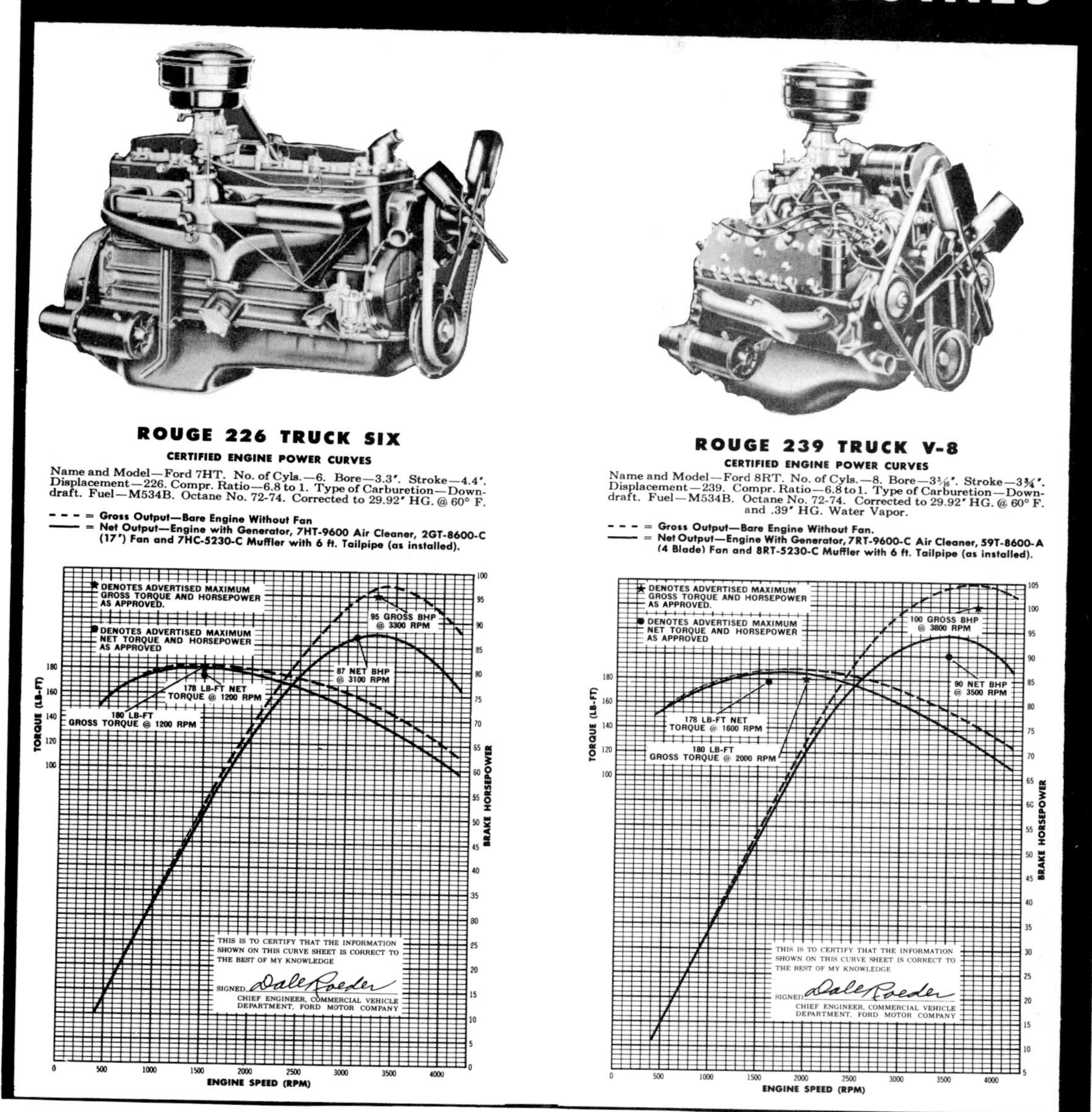

A 1949 comparison of the Rouge 226 six and the Rouge 239 V-8.

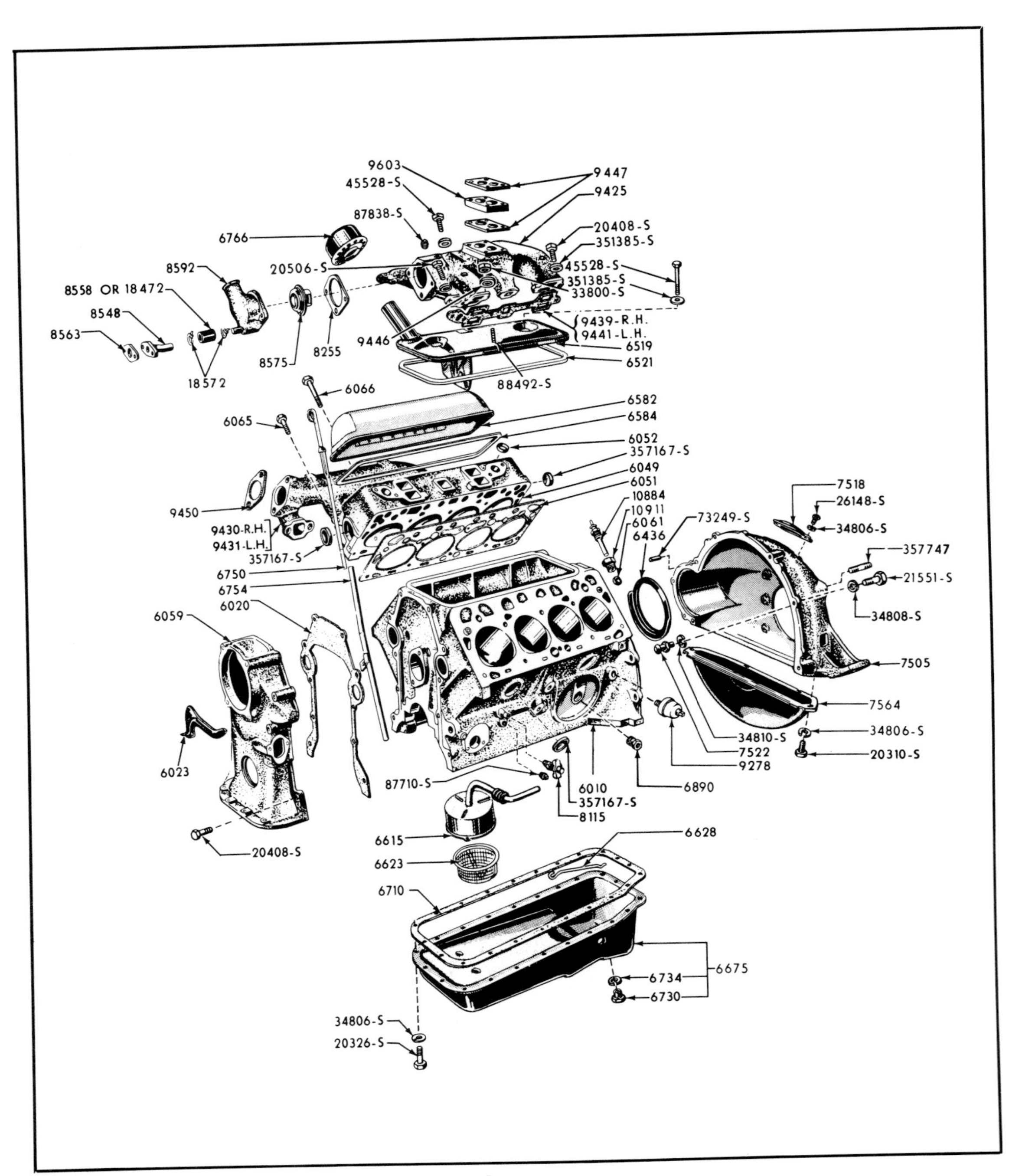

Typical cylinder block assembly for the Ford overhead valve V-8 fitted to the truck series. Details will change from engine type to engine type.

Parts sources

The following list of parts sources should give you an idea where to turn if you need help locating parts for your special truck. Your Ford dealer's parts department still carries a lot of parts for these trucks, so check there first. If you can't find what you need there, contact one or more of the suppliers listed here. These venders cater to the needs of the 1948-56 Ford truck enthusiast. Most carry the parts that Ford dealers carry plus some they don't.

Arizona
Arizona F-100 Parts
5230 W. Luke, #2
Glendale, AZ 85301
(602) 842-4280
specializes in new, NOS, used, and reproduction parts and accessories

California
Accent Interiors
P.O. Box 505
Yuba City, CA 95992
(916) 673-7426
carries interior kits and tonneau covers for 1953-56 Ford pickups

C & G Early Ford Parts
165 Balboa St. C-11
Mission Industrial Sq.
San Marcos, CA 92069
(619) 744-0470
carries new trim, body, rubber and mechanical parts for 1948-56 Ford trucks as well as earlier trucks and cars; illustrated catalog available

Clifford Research
15572 Computer Ln.
Huntington Beach, CA 92649
(714) 895-3887
specializes in high-performance intake and exhaust systems for Ford six-cylinders; catalog available

F-100 Ford Parts Unlimited
280 E. Jackson
San Jose, CA 95116
(408) 292-F100
carries 1948 and later truck parts, mostly NOS; specializes in 1953-56 F-100s

Sacramento Vintage Ford Parts
1504 El Camino Ave.
Sacramento, CA 95815
(916) 922-3444
carries a complete line of 1948-60 truck parts; free catalog

So-Cal Pickups Inc.
6412 Manchester Blvd.
Buena Park,CA 90621
(714) 994-1400 or (213) 941-4693
specializes in stock and custom parts for 1953-56 Ford F-100s; starting to carry parts for 1948-52 F-1s and later-model F-100s; illustrated catalog available

Truck Stop
1477 N. Carolan
Burlingame, CA 94010
(415) 344-4117

Valley Ford Parts
11610 Vanowen St.
N. Hollywood, CA 91605
(818) 982-5303
carries new, used, NOS and reproduction parts; catalog available

Vintage Auto Parts Inc.
402 W. Chapman Ave.
Orange, CA 92666
(714) 538-1130
offers new, NOS and reproduction parts

W. C. Trucking
821 Lytle St.
Redlands, CA 92374
(714) 794-6608
carries 1953-56 door panels, dash repair panels and other parts

Georgia
Obsolete Ford Parts Co.
311 E. Washington Ave.
Nashville, GA 31639
(912) 686-2470
offers a full line of parts for 1948-72 Ford pickups; new, used, NOS and reproductions; catalog #1 covering 1948-56 available

Renaissance Automotive
Terry Hulsey
548 Rivercrest Dr.
Woodstock, GA 30188
carries used parts for 1948-52 Ford F-1 trucks

Illinois
Rock Valley Antique Auto Parts
Route 72 at Rothwell Rd.
Stillman Valley, IL 61804
(815) 645-2271
carries only a few Ford truck parts for the 1948-56 era such as steel running boards, tail-light arms

Kansas
Cornelius Ford Parts
Dan Cornelius
3343 N. 61st St.
Kansas City, KS 66104
(913) 334-2881
specializes in new 1942-60 truck parts; some are genuine NOS, some are reproductions or replacement parts from other suppliers; catalog available

Rick's Antique Auto Parts
2754 Roe Ln.
Kansas City, KS 66103
(800) 255-4100
offers some reproduction parts for 1948-65 Ford trucks; catalog available

Kentucky
The Ford Parts Warehouse
Courthouse Sq.
Liberty, KY 42539
(606) 787-5031
carries NOS parts

Maryland
Anderson Industries Inc.
6599 Washington Blvd.
Elkridge, MD 21227
(301) 796-4382
carries fiberglass body parts; catalog available

Michigan
Muscle Parts
P.O. Box 2579
Dearborn, MI 48123
(800) 922-3400

Minnesota
Little Dearborn Parts
2424 University Ave.
Minneapolis, MN 55414
(612) 331-2066
carries new, NOS and reproduction parts

Missouri
Mack Products
Box 278
Moberly, MO 65270
carries reproduction parts for Ford pickups

Nevada
Bob's Classic Auto Glass
341 A Moran St.
Reno, NV 89502
(800) 624-2130
offers clear, tinted and smoked glass for Ford vehicles

New York
Joblot Automotive
98-11 211th St.
Queens Village
Long Island, NY 11429
(212) 468-8585
carries parts and accessories for 1948-64 Ford trucks, mostly mechanical; some body parts and literature; catalog available

North Carolina
Dan Carpenter
Rt. 2 Box 390AA
Norwood, NC 28128
(704) 474-3842
manufactures sheet metal parts for pickup beds

Dennis Carpenter Ford Reproductions
P.O. Box 26398
Charlotte, NC 28213
(704) 786-8139
famous for exact factory reproductions of Ford plastic and rubber parts as well as a full line of new parts for 1932-60 Ford pickups; catalog available

Oklahoma
Obsolete Ford Parts Inc.
6601 S. Shields
Oklahoma City, OK 73149
(405) 631-3933
carries full lines of parts and literature for 1948-60 Ford trucks

Oregon
Bob Drake Reproductions
1819 N.W. Washington Blvd.
Grants Pass, OR 97526
(800) 221-3673
specializes in reproductions, especially rubber items; catalog available

Bud's F-100 Parts
945 La Salle St.
Harrisburg, OR 97446
(503) 995-6466

Wisconsin
Modine Manufacturing Co.
1500 Dekoven Ave.
Racine, WI 53401
(414) 636-1200
offers replacement radiators

Old Time Auto Parts Inc.
2741 Highway N.
Cottage Grove, WI 53527
(608) 873-8646
carries new parts for 1928-56 Ford vehicles; catalog #4 covering 1948-56 Ford pickups available

Canada
Mercury Madness
24898 56th Ave.
Aldergrove, British Columbia
Canada V0X 1A0
specializes in parts for Ford and Mercury trucks of this era

Clubs

The Early Ford V-8 Club of America
P.O. Box 2122
San Leandro, CA 94577

Recognizes all Ford Motor Company vehicles produced from 1932 through 1953, basically the flathead years. One of the largest clubs of its kind, with over 8,000 members and 120 affiliated chapters. Restoration to stock specifications is stressed, but all Ford enthusiasts are welcomed. Hosts shows and meets on national, regional and local levels. Produces an excellent magazine that caters to the early Ford V-8 enthusiast.

The Light Commercial Vehicle Association
c/o Irvin Neubert
Route 14 Box 468
Jonesboro, TN 37659

For all enthusiasts who favor light commercial vehicles. Produces a nice bimonthly magazine that is full of trucking information covering all years. Also maintains a complete library and has a staff of technical advisers to help members with questions and problems.

Fabulous Fifties Ford Club of America
P.O. Box 286
Riverside, CA 92502

Open to all 1949-60 Ford Motor Company products and enthusiasts. National club with regional chapters located throughout the United States. Besides publications, the club sponsors national, regional and local meets throughout the year.

Ford/Mercury Club of America
P.O. Box 3551
Hayward, CA 94540

Open to all Ford Motor Company products from 1941 through 1953. Over 1,000 members and regional chapters. Bimonthly publication.

Performance Ford Club of America
P.O. Box 32
Ashville, OH 43103

Open to all Ford Motor Company vehicles, stock or modified, and their enthusiasts. Regional chapters located throughout the US. Produces excellent bimonthly magazine, *The Ford Enthusiast*.

Ford Pick-Ups Limited of Southern California
Burbank Chapter
P.O. Box 6252
Burbank, CA 91505

Local chapters are open to 1953-56 pickup owners. Family-oriented club that enjoys car shows, truck runs, picnics and so on. Trucks may be stock or modified.

Reader's page

If you liked reading this book and would like to read other books covering Ford trucks, I can recommend the following titles:

Ford Trucks Since 1905
By James K. Wagner, Crestline Publishing. This book covers Ford trucks since before the Ford Motor Company was officially in the truck business. Prior to 1920, Ford trucks were actually Ford cars modified with truck kits provided by outside suppliers. Many pictures and some text make for entertaining reading.

The Ford Y-Block, Origin-Maintenance-Rebuild
By James Eickman, Motorbooks International. A guide to Ford's first ohv V-8 engine, the successor to the venerable flattie.

Illustrated History of Ford
By George H. Dammann, Crestline Publishing. Same format as Wagner's book, with lots of photographs and some text. Many good photographs of Ford trucks from the early teens through 1970. Ford cars are also covered through 1970.

Pickup and Van Spotters Guide 1945-1982
By Tad Burness, Motorbooks International. This is a guide that enthusiasts can use to help identify trucks. Burness uses photographs and clippings from sales materials, plus much specification data. This informal approach makes for an easy-to-read, easy-to-use book.

Truckin'
If you are a truck enthusiast, you are going to enjoy this monthly magazine. It covers all years of pickups, vans and so on, including subjects that are very appealing to enthusiasts of older trucks. It covers material that will be of value to restorers, also catering to the needs of the truck rodder. Available at newsstands or by subscription.